. . . now I find myself

in a new country, surrounded by

objects entirely strange. The people

lead a careless and sauntering life.

Goethe
Travels in Italy

NEW ORLEANS
UNMASQUED

NEW ORLEANS UNMASQUED

Being A

Wagwit's Sketches

of a Singular American City

by

S. FREDERICK STARR

drawings by

FRANKLIN ADAMS

édition dedeaux
NEW ORLEANS, NEW YORK

DEDICATION

Fat Tuesday: Marching to a Different Drummer

These Sketches Are Dedicated To
The Three Great New Orleans Portraitists:

Lafcadio Hearn
Essayist
(1800 - 1904)

Clarence John Laughlin
Surrealist Photographer
(1905 - 1985)

Danny Barker
Jazz Musician and Historian
(1909 -   )

New Orleans UnMasqued:
Being A Wagwit's Affectionate Sketches
Of A Singular American City

Copyright © 1985 by S. Frederick Starr

é d i t i o n   d e d e a u x
Dedeaux Publishing Incorporated
Post Office Box Number 70406
New Orleans, Louisiana 70172

Library of Congress Catalog Number:
    84-072514

ISBN: 0-930987-00-4 (case)
        0-930987-01-2 (paper)

Design: Xariffa Atelier
Typesetting: Studio G
Manufactured in the United States of America

TABLE OF CONTENTS

Chapter XV: **Politics,** *continued*

Chapter XVI: **An Earnest Epilogue**

ILLUSTRATIONS

A FRIVOLOUS PROLOGUE

*In which the reader's global vision
is narrowed to just one spot, on the ground that,
as Ruskin put it,
"He who can take no interest in what is small
will take false interest
in what is great."*

A Question of depth of field.

A FRIVOLOUS PROLOGUE

This book is about a city situated in North America at 29° 56' north latitude and 90° 84' west longtitude. From orbiting satellites it can be discerned, barely, as a faint discoloration near the mouth of the Mississippi, a kind of nicotine stain on the bearded delta of the Great River. Astronomers assure us that this city, like everything else on earth, is whirling around the polar axis at nearly a thousand miles an hour, all day every day. This fact belies the claim that New Orleans is standing still.

Far from it! The city is alive with motion. It bubbles and chugs with energy like a tea kettle just before the whistle sounds. People here are buying, selling, investing their resources and laying waste their powers. Market researchers consider New Orleans the thirty-fourth best city for advertising in the United States. There is no want of motion. But a keen observer peering downward from the height of a balloon—and people have sought out this vantage point above the table-flat city for a century—would notice that the motion is not linear but, instead, describes a circle. Many circles, actually, intricate curlicues of interwoven scrollwork, like the ornate flourishes of Victorian penmanship.

Among the world's cities, New Orleans is very young. On the young continent of North America, however, it is considered old. Nearing three centuries, it one of the few American cities to have what uninformed observers mistake for "charm." Undeniably, it has a personality—one that was discernable almost from the first moment Europeans began to swat mosquitos on Bayou St. John. Since then, that personality has been carefully aged, like a big old cheese. Decades of solitude helped the process, although now the city is being yanked back into the mainstream, slightly dazed, to be sure, like a wallflower who has sat out three dances and is suddenly asked to tango.

There is much about New Orleans that is, if not charming, at least quaint or comic. There is much, too, that is quite literally absurd, i.e., illogical, contrary to all reason or common sense, dissonant. Now, absurdity, as Nabokov observed, comes in many flavors. Some absurdity can be dismissed with a smile or a shrug. Other absurdity touches on lofty aspirations, strong passions, and deep despair. New Orleans' absurdity fits both types. As such, it is bound to stimulate thought—although not too much.

This book defends no learned thesis. It does not, for example, offer a decisive refutation (by now the one hundred and sixty-first) of H. L. Mencken's character-ization of the American South as "The Sahara of the Beaux Arts." Such arguments have a cunning way of providing support, unwittingly, for precisely the opposite view from the one they seek to defend.

Nor does it provide some lofty moral lesson. If it were to propose, for instance, that the American character would be improved by a dash of good old Mediterranean Catholic indolence, rest assured that thousands of do-gooders would take this up as their cause, and pursue it with an utter lack of sloth. Meetings and rallies would be held, organizations formed, and drafting commissions convened to implement the idea. Soon massive programs would be inculcating an ethic of dynamic indolence in every schoolroom in the land, a kind of *McGuffy's Reader* approach to sloth. It would never work.

Far from serving up learned theses or moral lessons, this book offers nothing more than casual impressions. In the old days before George Eastman's Brownie cameras arrived on the scene, the seasoned traveler kept a sketchbook. Whenever the mood struck him he would haul out his traveling desk, usually an elegant little box of mahogany or cherry with leather-lined compartments for paper, ink, and pens. Materials in hand, he would then immortalize the scene before him. The following vignettes are the written versions of such amateur sketches.

Like the drawings of an old-time traveler, these written souvenirs offer a view that is limited by the author's own eyes. In a photograph, people and objects may slip into the background, unobserved at the moment of the shutter's click. These become surprises to be pondered over brandy and cigars by the puzzled photographer when he shares the pictures with friends in his study. But in the case of sketches, whatever the sketcher misses is missed. The lacunae reveal the author no less surely than do the sketches. It is probably for this reason that the English philanthropist and utopian crank, Robert Owen, is said to have avoided reading travel literature. Instead, he confined his attention to statistical studies and census reports. The reader may well decide to follow Owen's lead.

There is one further resemblance that these vignettes bear to an old sketchbook: they were written for family and a handful of friends, rather than for some hypothetical reader who charges the book on his VISA card and proceeds to read his purchase while traveling the New York subway. Picture him, with one raised hand grasping for the oily metal handle of the IRT as it crashes over the switches under Columbus Circle, and with the other hand clutching this unlikely book. That same reader might later be tempted to take in hand his portable recorder and dictate a letter to the publisher correcting some detail on the basis of what he has heard from his brother-in-law, who works for Howard, Weil, Labouisse and Friedrichs in New Orleans. Let him save his energy. Better, let him start his own collection of sketches of Bronxville, or of Westport, or Hopewell. The field is large.

The fact that these vignettes were written for so limited an audience may explain why there is an absence of formal acknowledgements. But warm thanks are due many people, especially those dear friends and acquaintances in the Crescent City who frequent the same haunts as does the author and who practice the nearly lost art of smiling at themselves.

S. Frederick Starr
New Orleans, Louisiana

BRAVE NEW WORLD

*In which some forces of change in New Orleans
are introduced, and in which the City's curious
relationship to just about everywhere else
is duly noted.*

A girl who can't say no

BRAVE NEW WORLD

New Orleans is built on mush, literally. The recipe calls for 200 feet of the best alluvial soil washed in from Minnesota, Nebraska, and Pennsylvania. Then soak the soil in water from the same sources to form a smooth, stratified pudding. No granite fundament lies beneath this, either. Instead, there is a layer of compacted sand just hard enough, with luck, to support a building.

These formidable obstacles have, until recently, imposed a welcome modesty on New Orleans architects. Down to the past decade the boldest attempt to tackle the mush problem was made in the 1850's, when the U.S. Customs House was allegedly planted on submerged bales of cotton. Such bales were appealingly organic and indigenous, and marked the outer limit of grandomania in architecture—until now.

The pudding problem has finally been conquered by the 100-ton American crane equipped with a vulcan 80 C pile driving hammer. Cotton bales now give way to 190-foot long prestressed concrete pilings, each capable of bearing a 400-ton design load. Enough of these concrete fingers driven into the earth can support the 56-story Place St. Charles.

The sound is deafening and relentless. On any day, the Binnings Construction Company, Inc., and S.K. Whitty and Company, Inc. post an arsenal of half a dozen drivers up and down the length of Poydras Street. Like Prometheus, who stole fire from the gods, these machines have transformed New Orleans' relationship to nature. The old limits are gone. And yet, New Orleans is a city that was defined by the limits that nature imposed upon it. Nature proscribed certain building types, certain clothes, certain foods, a certain way of life. Human beings—at least, those who wished to survive—accommodated these demands the way ancient Greek playwrights accommodated the demand that only three actors occupy the stage at once. By recognizing the limits and working creatively within them, New Orleanians created something unique.

The limits do not exist now. Much to the relief of megalomaniacal architects, nature no longer calls the tune. But, one might wonder, is the music of the new Poydras Street worth singing?

HOUSTON

"I've been to the Future and it is Houston." With these words, *Figaro*, a New Orleans weekly, named the spectre haunting New Orleans from the West. *Figaro* is now defunct. The spectre is still real.

It is easy to denigrate Houston from the security of Canal Street. "A cluster of Shreveports," as one New Orleanian put it; "All highways and no byways," says another. But Houston is not so glibly dismissed. Its Petroleum Club is to New Orleans what Captain Ahab was to your typical weekend angler. At least one of the new glass boxes on Poydras Street is an exact duplicate of a prototype in Texas. New Orleans' new skyscrapers are, as a *New York Times* critic put it "intrusions," "full of anxiety, nervousness and pretension." In a word, Houston is the city we love to hate.

But Houston just loves New Orleans, finds it cute. It buys up New Orleans real estate the way Saudi sheiks buy castles in England. New Orleans is to Houston as Vienna is to Berlin, Rome to Milan: old, charming, irrelevant, a good time.

Will New Orleans be Houstonized? It nearly happened in 1965, when the Louisiana Highway Department proposed to build an expressway along the Mississippi River right through the Vieux Carre. Amazingly, the New Orleans Chamber of Commerce took up the idea, seeing the 90 percent federal funding as a bargain. The leading paper rhapsodized over it. Eventually, the idea was killed. There remains a monument to this folly, however, a section of echo-filled tunnel that runs under the Rivergate Exhibition Center. Thwarted in the air, Houston burrowed nearly to the Vieux Carre.

That same year, Houston opened its $38,000,000 Astrodome. New Orleans counter-punched, this time scoring a knock-out. The Louisiana Superdome out-Houstons Houston. Not only is its seating capacity half again larger than the Astrodome's and its price tag four times greater, but it is the biggest enclosed space on the planet, covering nine acres. On a good night the Superdome attracts enough people to consume 22,000 hot dogs, 75,000 cups of beer, and 50,000 sodas. It has eighty-eight restrooms.

It is rumored that Houston is preparing to build its own French Quarter, complete with ten-gallon strippers.

T O U R I S T S

The population of New Orleans is over one-half million. Each year another seven million people trek to the Crescent City as tourists. More than two hundred hotels and motels provide some 24,000 guest rooms to accommodate this invasion. An army of nearly a thousand women is required just to make the beds. Fortunately, the tourists bring money, and the city obliges by offering many attractions to spend it on.

Each tourist also carries with him an image of the place he is visiting. Once *in situ,* he determinedly sets out to discover in New Orleans living embodiments of that image. The Midwesterner prowls around for pure, unsullied jazz played "the way it was before it went up the river to Chicago." (Indiana schools, apparently, teach that Chicago is on the Mississippi.) Earnest Scandinavians, their faces beet-red from the summer's heat, seek out Louis Armstrong and Jelly Roll Morton on every corner. And Frenchmen arrive expecting to hear the language of Voltaire, carelessly forgetting that Napoleon denied them that convenience by selling off Louisiana in 1803.

Each tourist finds precisely what he expected to find, contented at having made contact with "the real New Orleans." The "real New Orleans," meanwhile, smugly revels in its privacy.

P L A S T I C

The Desire Bar is tucked into the modern brick mass of the Royal Sonesta Hotel on Bourbon Street at Bienville. In order to build the hotel they had first to tear down a brewery and a number of fine old Creole homes. The hole was so deep that it caused land in the entire area to shift, which threatened the collapse of several more ancient buildings fronting on Royal Street.

The design of the hotel exudes the 1960's, but the Desire Bar evokes another era. In a breathtaking transposition, its walls are decorated with framed photographs of the old Vieux Carre—in fact, pictures of the very buildings that were pulled down to make way for the hotel. Here, at the point zero of historic New Orleans, the plasticized image has replaced reality.

Other national hotel chains have followed a similar course. Accountants have assured developers that modern high-rise hotels are the greatest achievement in architecture since the Parthenon. But to pin their creations to the reality of Louisiana, the developers in Los Angeles or New York love nothing better than to build into them *ersatz* Bourbon Street bars, gaudy with plush and complete with live jazz bands. Such watering holes are not one but two steps from reality, being plastic imitations of bars that are themselves plastic imitations of romanticized Storyville saloons of yesteryear.

This triumph of image over reality occurred early in New Orleans. Long before the invention of plastic, in 1726 to be exact, French boosters of the Louisiana colony decided to gather some of their local color to impress the folks in Paris. Since New Orleans had barely been founded, they turned to Indians from farther up the river. The native Louisianians were scrubbed up, dressed in what Frenchmen thought Indians should wear, and packed off to Versailles. Over in the Bois de Boulogne these living ads for tourism hunted deer, roped horses, and put on the world's first Wild West Show. The French court was delighted; meanwhile, as plasticized Indians were cavorting at Versailles, real Indians were becoming scarcer every day.

There are purists who fear that the "real" New Orleans is vanishing, or that it has already vanished. But did it ever exist? Bourbon Street may be a plasticized version of Storyville, but Storyville itself was pure fantasy, its fake oriental *seraglios* recalling splendors that never were. But what about those elegant drawing rooms on aristocratic Esplanade Avenue or in the Garden District? Surely *these* were real? Alas, these, too, were created as fanciful imitations of Parisian townhouses and Tuscan villas that few New Orleanians had ever seen. But that does not make them a whit less authentic. Plastic was not invented yesterday . . . and it, too, is real.

OUTPOST

New Orleans is not isolated. Ships from nations unknown to all but the readers of the most recent edition of the *Encyclopedia Britannica* steam into its port. Jumbo jets and interstate highways inundate the city with visitors. And the Crescent City can even be reached by railroad, or by what passes for a railroad in the Amtrak era.

Paris and Venice, too, are thronged with visitors and derive much economic benefit from them. Don't mistake the tourists' world for true local life in those cities, however. Whatever indigenous society still exists in Paris and Venice survives by distancing itself from the tourists' gaze, as if to say "we will still be here when you all go home, so leave us alone." Such distancing also occurs in New Orleans, where it is systematic. At all levels, the indigenous community maintains its existence separate from (though sometimes parallel to) that of the tourists' micro-habitat. More than one restaurant even has a separate door for its regular local patrons (doors formerly used by gentlemen for their most discreet entertaining). If you by chance come across that door at Antoine's, don't flatter yourself with the thought that you have "arrived." Just try getting one of Antoine's "local" waiters to help you if your home base is Minneapolis. You'll quickly understand.

The flight of New Orleanians into their separate world is quite natural, but it is reinforced by the city's cultural isolation on the North American continent. New Orleans was founded from the seas, as a northern outpost of the Caribbean world. French and Catholic, New Orleans looked north to a hinterland populated by Anglo-Saxons and Protestants who spoke a different language, both literally and figuratively. The distance between New Orleans and northern Louisiana (forget the rest of the country) ran as wide and as deep as the English Channel. No true New Orleanian is surprised when, on one of his rare forays into the hinterland, he encounters towns with names like China, Lisbon, Elba, Arizona, Poland or Lebanon. It is a different world out there.

Viewed from the snug perspective of upper Canal Street, the nation beyond the city limits appears like the western seas in the work of a fifteenth-century cartographer—the very heart of darkness, inhabited by nameless monsters, by "them." In the old days "they" were foul-mouthed and foul-smelling keelboatmen from "Kaintuck." After the Civil War "they" appeared again, this time as carpetbaggers eager to make a quick buck in the only southern city to have escaped destruction in the fighting. During the 1920's and 1930's the "they" who counted were practically neighbors, Louisianians who spoke with a strange drawl and hailed from the Baptist parishes in the north of the state. Led by Huey Long and his red-necked backers, "they" all bore a grudge against the Crescent City for its relative wealth, its aloofness and its purported moral decadence. Today "they" are wheeler-dealers from Texas, California and just about everywhere else, all of them eager to buy a piece of the action on the slick new Poydras Street.

Because of "them," New Orleanians have, quite reasonably, tended to view themselves as being "under siege," which is exactly what a local state senator argued in Baton Rouge last year. Like Romans in the fifth century A.D., denizens of the Crescent City try to fend off the barbarian hordes while at the same time picking their pockets, literally as well as figuratively. Such a history has made New Orleanians somewhat introverted and self-preoccupied, not unlike the population of the Hanseatic port of Lübeck as described by Thomas Mann in his epic novel *Buddenbrooks.*

Yet for all this, New Orleanians can also be extraordinarily hospitable, as millions of tourists can attest. The hospitality is genuine, but "they" still try the City's patience at times. As sport fans or rock music enthusiasts pour into the Superdome from the small towns of northern Louisiana and Mississippi, the ring of cash registers is like the sweetest music to local ears. The yokels gaze upward in awe at the Superdome's vast roof, with its rubbery skin of hypalon and insulation of polyurethane. They order another beer, then another. Finally, the "good ol' boys" get back into their pickups and Caddies and, as they speed away on the I-10, exuberantly riddle the roof of the Dome with parting blasts from their magnums. The bill for repairing the roof's skin hit $4.5 million last year. Such statistics make the fading taillights look not all bad to New Orleanians.

HABITS

III

*In which diverse local habits,
some of ancient origins, are enumerated,
leading to the suggestion that everything
in New Orleans may not be changing after all.*

Carnival Flambeau: Eternal Flame

HABITS

Some practices continue from the past in New Orleans because they have been labeled as traditions. Such are the reeling steps performed by the *flambeaux* carriers in the nocturnal Carnival parades. The floats themselves are now pulled by tractors instead of mules. Tractors foul the air rather than the street. And they are not, well, mulish. But the way is still lit by sputtering *flambeaux,* carried proudly aloft by black sons and grandsons of those who carried them in the past. And the shuffling dance step that these sweating *flambeaux* carriers perform is nothing less than the cakewalk, frozen in tradition since the 1890's.

Many other local practices in New Orleans persist through unconscious habit. On Monday the Lord created the firmament, and on subsequent Mondays New Orleanians have eaten red beans and rice. Professors of nutrition have written dissertations in praise of this simple dish. And well they might. Alone, each element is hardly worth discussing. In tandem they shoot vitamins and proteins into your body like grandma's cod-liver oil. *Chaurice,* the hot local sausage introduced by the Spaniards, just adds flavor.

But this is not why New Orleanians stick to red beans and rice. If nutrition were the issue, they would be eating health foods as well, which is decidedly not the case. Rather, the one-two punch of beans and rice entered the local cuisine because it could survive the summer heat. Both the beans and the rice could be dried and safely stored. The ham bone and sausage were smoked. As a result, this was one of the few dishes that one could eat in the steamy summer without fear of poisoning. Beans and rice are also easily prepared, the perfect dish for wash day, which was Monday.

Notice that all the objective reasons for eating red beans and rice have now changed. Refrigerators enable us to eat safely any dish in any season. Home washing machines destroyed the Monday work ritual, and wiped out the National Washboard Company in the process. There is no practical necessity for eating red beans and rice any more, unless you're hooked on them.

Many New Orleanians are addicted, and so they continue to boil up their beans and rice out of sheer habit. To meet the demand, even the most impersonal supermarket chains are forced to stock whole aisles of beans and rice. The Winn-Dixie store in St. Bernard finds it virtually impossible to move red meat, Boston lettuce, broccoli, or artichokes. But it sells beans and rice by the ton. And Tabasco sauce. And *chaurice.* An expert on the local food industry estimates that 350,000 servings of beans and rice were being offered up each week in the early 1980's. That's four times as many as in Boston, which pretends to the title of "Beantown."

COMMUNICATIONS

It is said that New Orleans is not a news town. In one sense it's not, for it supports only one daily paper, the nobly titled *Times-Picayune*. Actually, the name of the paper is far grander even than this. When the English Crown swallowed Wales and Scotland, it added the royal titles of those provinces to its own; for the same reason, New Orleans' one newspaper bears the full title of *The Times-Picayune-The States-Item*. As in so many other American cities, the paper's masthead reads like a list of martyrs on a war memorial.

The death of all but one city-wide daily paper does not alone prove that New Orleans is a bad town for news, nor does the fact that New Orleans imports fewer copies of *Newsweek* or *The New York Times* per capita than do most American cities of similar size. Rather, such facts remind us that in New Orleans, newsprint can scarcely compete with the proverbial backyard fence for sheer speed and depth of local coverage. "We don't have to read the paper to find out *what* happened," a local savant explains. "We read the paper to find out who got caught for doing it."

On human interest stories, the print media aren't even in the picture. Last Fourth of July, for example, *The Times Picayune* alleged that a certain Sam Pizzuto of Oleander Street had been booked for simple battery because "he punched his seventy-eight year-old mother, Antoinette Pizzuto, several times in an argument over money for a utility bill and the fact that the victim had thrown away her son's hot tamales." Clearly, only half the story is recorded herein. Were the tamales really hot? Or too hot? And why was Sam P.'s utility bill so high? Rest assured that everyone within a ten-block radius of Oleander Street scooped *The Times-Picayune*'s answers to these vital questions.

New Orleanians of all colors, rich or poor, are not content with mere facts. They want to plumb the motives, get behind the news. They have more contact with each other and know one another far better than do the citizenry of most American cities. As a result, their notions on causation in human affairs are more sophisticated than those of, say, Portlanders or Atlantans. Action "Z" may be the result of action "Y," as the newspaper proposed, but it may equally be a consequence of "X," "W," and all the way back to "A." What mere journalist can follow such subtle chains of cause and effect? It is scarcely surprising that Dorothy Dix, who counseled millions on the handling of everyday problems, did her homework in her adopted city of New Orleans.

Then there is gossip. Whether or not the Big Story is in the news, it is carried instantly over the lines of South Central Bell. In connection with the planning of a new ballet company, a large and particularly important meeting was held. Somehow the newspaper managed not to cover it. But never mind. Within a few days *Times-Picayune* columnists were alluding to the "well-known" meeting without elaboration, confident that the meeting was, in fact, well-known.

Such examples suggest that the telephone in New Orleans may constitute the most sophisticated cable news network in the entire country. It matters little that grossly erroneous stories sometimes go unchecked or that people who should know better repeat them. In the long run, the system is self-correcting.

And there is a long run. Edgar Degas, the French painter, spent time in New Orleans with his mother's family in the 1870s. So did his brother, René, who, in addition to becoming a cotton broker, made off with a neighbor's wife, America Olivier. It goes without saying that the local papers never reported this caper. But over a century later, when Edgar's name came up at a local dinner party, an octogenarian present rued that it was "such a pity that René brought shame on himself and his family." *That* was still news. His brother Edgar's daubings on canvas were not.

PUBLIC RELATIONS

Futurists assure us that the "age of information" is dawning. Standing atop reams of computer printout, they claim that our nation, which once produced iron, steel, and its own motorcycles, now has information as its chief product. Wall Street seems to agree. The communication industry booms, with advertising and public relations joining in the process.

New Orleans is charging headlong into this Brave New World. Communicators communicate to the community through a variety of media. Ambitious business and cultural groups hire PR pros to tell their tales. New ventures make their debuts at press conferences and the mayor himself promotes a task force to study New Orleans' image nationally.

But notice this: nearly all of New Orleans' communicators, ad-men, PR folk and media boosters are imports. Go to any meeting of true believers in these fields and you will hear the accents of Manhattan, The Loop, LA, or Boston—not the Ninth Ward, the Garden District or anywhere between. For the true child of Bienville's city knows in his guts that ballyhoo is bad and to be avoided. That's why the Advertising Club of New Orleans has only 250 members, while those in Baltimore,

Milwaukee, Columbus, and Memphis have well over 300. With only four large PR firms, the advertising business in New Orleans is still a cottage industry.

Now, if you must advertise, why should you turn the job over to some vulgar professional when you can do it yourself? The home brewed TV ad is a New Orleans specialty, an art form of sorts. A few local businessmen who tout their own products—Al Scramuzza of Seafood City, for example—turn into garrulous hams when the TV camera is on them. Most just stand there stolidly in their rumpled Haspel suits and tell you that their pianos, autos, or aluminum sidings are worth buying. Period. This no-nonsense approach to advertising reaches its zenith in the slogan employed by a local root beer company: "Drink Barq's. It's Good."

Along Gravier Street, even those who accept PR as a necessary evil believe that the best publicity is none at all. When an immigrant Babbitt suggests that his firm or organization should announce its new policy publicly, locally-bred colleagues respond with puzzled frowns. "It's nobody's business but ours." And so it isn't.

Long-time students of this cult of silence claim that it is a Creole legacy, a manifestation of the same passion for privacy that brought the poker bluff to its highest level in New Orleans. More likely, it is simply the most rational tactic for a commercial class that experienced a full century of hardship between the fall of King Cotton and the rise of Sheik Yamani. No news was good news.

At times, the cult of silence attains truly lofty heights. More than one New Orleans board has heatedly debated an issue for hours, only to vote afterwards that all mention of the discussion, and even of the vote, be struck from the minutes. And what politician, businessman, or civic leader has not had a colleague conclude a *tête à tête* with the words, "This conversation did not take place"?

PHONETICS

The first problem one encounters in dealing with the Crescent City is pronouncing its name. In Standard American it's NuORlins. In Southern Standard it's rendered as NooAHLinz. Nee-yew Or-LEENZ is also popular, possibly because the lyrics for several tunes about the city call for this pronunciation, which is surely why Nu-WALnz native Louis Amstrong switched over to it. Most locals, in fact, opt for this compressed form: NuWALnz. But uptown you will make out four distinct syllables, each clipped, and with nearly equal stress: Noo OR-li-unz.

Can these difficulties of pronunciation be blamed on the fact that half of the city's name is French? To some extent, yes. Crescent City natives still use several French terms in everyday speech, but they mispronounce them all. The *batture* along the Mississippi is called the BATCHer, while the *banquette* by the side of the street is known as the BANKit. An otherwise capable local politico named Faucheux imaginatively reworked his own name into Fo-shay.

But the *Franglais* problem constitutes only one aspect of the phonetic hodge-podge that is New Orleans. Savor these samples of common pronunciations from the Crescent City:

sundi	-	Sunday
areddi	-	already
indivijli	-	individually
sinANtree	-	St. Anthony
kontrak	-	contract
prolly	-	probably
chirrin	-	children
charridy	-	charity
semiNAR	-	St. Bernard
innepenint	-	independent
zink	-	sink
woik	-	work
fwoist	-	first
dawlin	-	darling

Some of these gems, characteristic of the city's old Third and Ninth Wards, reveal that peculiar New Orleans drawl that casual observers mistake for Brooklynese. In order to keep the linguists on their toes, this accent follows no simple rules. Thus, the name "Earl" is pronounced "Oil," but the stuff you pour in the crank case of your car is "Erl." It's all very puzzling.

Here, by contrast, are some samples gathered on the streets of uptown New Orleans, the last bastion of the pert pronunciation of the city's name as Noo OR-li-unz or Noo ORL-yuns. Reading them, it is worth recalling that in the old Creole *patois* of New Orleans the letter "r" was never sounded:

wud	-	word
shooa	-	sure
kawa	-	car
fawdi-aid	-	forty-eight
fuwst	-	first
upbah	-	upper

New Orleans may be a cosmopolitan place, but no foreign word ever survived there for more than a week without being thoroughly reconstituted. The Spaniards *Calaboza* became "calaboose"; the French *Chartres* became "Charters"; *Hotel Dieu* becomes "Hotel Doo." Could it be possible that New Orleanians' mouths contain uniquely configured pharyngeal cavities, uvulas of remarkable design, or vela that reshape each sound?

The placing of accents is standardized throughout the English-speaking world— except in New Orleans. There, a violin is a VI-olin. Never mind that a name like Ulysses is well known under its standard Homer and U.S. Grant pronunciation. In New Orleans it's YOU-lisis. And the renowned Frenchman, de Lessups, the builder of the Suez Canal whose descendants are still very much in evidence in New Orleans? That's DELla-sups.

The accent problem is especially serious for place names. Copernicus Street is "CopperNICKus"; Burgundy Street is "BurGUNdy"; Milan Street is "MYlan." This makes for confusion among visitors to the city. In order to ease guests smoothly into New Orleans life, the Council would do well to adopt the ancient Greek or Sanskrit system for marking accents and use it on all street signs.

A convenient rule for New Orleanating even the most familiar words is to drop syllables whenever possible. Natives long ago discovered that this saves wear and tear on the jaw muscles. This simple process transforms Calliope Street into "CALiowp," the village of Metairie into "METry," Melpomene Street into "MELPmean," Terpsichore Street into "TURPsikor," and Socrates Street into "SOCKrats."

Words are commonly changed to suit the speaker's convenience or merely to satisfy his fancy. Ulloa Street is thus called "You-OWE-la," and Burthe Street is always pronounced "Byouth."

New Orleanians think nothing of renaming people as well, especially if they have the slightest difficulty pronouncing the name someone happened to have been given at birth. A likable Swede named Orjan came to town and quickly became "Orange," while a dignified visitor from Iceland by the name of Aknar was transformed by his New Orleanian co-workers into "Eggnog." Or take the Japanese businessman from the Kawai Watch Company whose name was deemed unpronounceable and who therefore became known to his New Orleans associates as "Kwatch," after his firm's Telex code.

Once you are renamed by New Orleanians, you're stuck. Rather than put up with what is bound to be futile resistance, it's best to change your name to fit the pronunciation. A family of immigrants came to the Crescent City a century and a half ago from the lovely Danubian city of Passau. The Passauers' bar soon became known as Parasols, which name is today emblazoned on the sign out front.

The very word "jazz" sprang from this process. A prostitute in the old days was called a "Jezebel," after the Old Testament usage. In New Orleans, this was soon shortened to "Jazzbel" or "Jazzbelle." A "Jazzbelle's" pimp or male sidekick was naturally a "Jazzbeau" or "Jazzbo." By the turn of the century, the music they danced to was being called "jazz."

CRYPTOLOGY

"Hey LiROY! Weah y'at?"
"AwWRITE, CHUbindooin?"
"NUTin...JEET jet?"
"Na, JEW?"

"Na, JEW?"
"Uhuh."
"Den KUMtadaERstrhas WIDme."
"AwRAeet!"

SUBURBS

Tourists arriving in New Orleans by air sometimes express shock at discovering that the French Quarter does not extend to the edge of Moisant (New Orleans International) Airfield's Runway No. 2. Instead, their refined sensibilities are forced to run the gauntlet of monotonous suburbs extending more than a dozen miles outward from the city. It is the Sun Belt at its worst. Here are the endless rows of restaurants, filling stations, and furniture marts backing on more endless rows of one-story housing and condominiums with phony mansard roofs. To all appearances, you could be in Tallahassee, on the fringe of Jackson, in Phoenix, or—perish the thought—in Houston.

Yet suburban New Orleans cannot be taken lightly. The per capita income there far outpaces that of New Orleans proper. The population of Jefferson Parish (the heart of Creole suburbia) more than doubled between 1960 and 1980. By contrast, the city of New Orleans lost population during those years.

Where did people go? Many old black Creole families from the Seventh Ward headed to the east, some to Pontchartrain Park, the first middle-class black subdivision, and others to new housing developments near the Interstate. Many whites also went east but most went west to Jefferson Parish, or south, to the confusingly named "West Bank."

It may not look it, but the suburbs are as thoroughly New Orleanian as Dorgenois Street. They have their own Mardi Gras krewes and their own family restaurants amidst the Burger Kings. And like those West Virginia mountaineers whose speech preserves elements of Elizabethan English that long ago dropped from use in London, suburban New Orleanians preserve intact the delicious accent of mid-town New Orleans of half a century ago. This is the so-called "Yat" dialect, which derives its name from the enigmatic query "Where y'at?" with which downtown residents of the Crescent City once greeted one another on the *banquette*.

The creation of the entertainment district "Fat City" in the 1960's marked a high point of suburbanization. Finally, suburban Jefferson Parish acquired its own genuine, true-to-life, nonbreakable, water-repellent, satisfaction-guaranteed Bourbon Street, complete with jazz joints, fine restaurants, massage parlors, and country and western bars. Fat City differs from the original Bourbon Street in three important aspects: its architecture is shopping-center modern; practically none of its habitués trace their genealogies to south of the Sahara; and as an entertainment center it is dying.

HOME TOWN NARCISSISM

Of Oakland, California, Gertrude Stein is said to have observed, "There is no There there." She was wrong, of course. Oakland has its own genuine people, streets, buildings, and memories of novelist Jack London. But who dreams of romantic escape to Oakland? Nobody. The Oakland Raiders themselves took flight to Los Angeles.

New Orleans is different, as Gertrude Stein learned when she went there to visit Sherwood Anderson. It is a There; it has an identity—several of them, in fact. Its inhabitants know it, and they revel in it.

No city in North America is more saturated with images of itself than New Orleans. Eight radio stations bombard the airways with pop music and jazz, the lyrics more often than not having the city of New Orleans and its people as the subject. Listening to your car radio, you can make a psychogeographical tour of the city, climbing up from "Basin Street Blues" or "West End Blues" to the giddy heights of "New Orleans Joys." It all induces a serene myopia, that comforting feeling of being embraced by one's home that big cities rarely afford.

Granted, the New Yorker can, in his less surly moods, sing "The Sidewalks of New York" in the shower, or belt out Cole Porter's upbeat testimonial, "I Happen to Like New York," or even Rodgers and Hart's "I'll Take Manhattan." Gotham, however, is simply too large and variegated to be comprehended with any single image, nor can it be a symbol of anything other than sheer size and its human consequences.

New Yorkers may be self-centered and, in their own way, provincial, but they haven't the slightest interest in the images with which others perceive them. Not so New Orleanians. One of the biggest news stories in recent years was the announcement by *Atlanta Magazine* that New Orleans has a future, and a very promising one at that. Big news, not because New Orleanians didn't know this to be the case, but because now Atlantans were saying it. Local narcissists swelled with pride.

The true narcissist doesn't need good news about himself. Any news will do. Older sports fans will recall the New Orleans Saints' long streak of losing seasons. At first it was mortifying. Then the narcissists realized that the performance of their team was so miserable that it brought them a certain reflected counter-glory. They wallowed in it, flaunting their humiliation by covering their heads with paper bags during the games. Everyone had a splendid time until the owners of the club brought in a new coach—named "Bum"—and the team started winning.

The pleasures of narcissism do not require an outside cheering section. They can be enjoyed in the privacy of one's home, or at the corner cinema. Take Tennessee Williams' *A Streetcar Named Desire*. The streetcar no longer runs, but a city bus still covers the route. *A Streetcar Named Desire* is also the 1951 film starring Marlon Brando and Vivian Leigh. This classic was recently shown in the Crescent City. Many local narcissists turned up just to watch Vivian Leigh's arrival at the old Union Station and her on-site trip through the city; most left when she arrived at her sister's studio-set house.

Is all this evidence of New Orleans' parochialism, of its lack of confidence in itself as a major city? Perhaps. Back in 1887 Charles Dudley Warner called New Orleans "the most cosmopolitan of provincial cities." Besides being demeaning, this assertion somewhat misses the point.

Far more accurate would be to say that New Orleans is the most provincial of cosmopolitan cities. And that's not all bad, either.

VISITING FIREMAN

Don't try to slip in and out of New Orleans unobserved, at least if you are an illustrious personage. It won't work. The normal run of people can do so easily enough, but it's quite impossible for the prominent and celebrated. For New Orleanians love to play host. They treasure the rituals of hospitality as the Japanese venerate their tea ceremonies. Since the rites associated with entertaining out-of-town visitors cannot proceed without the renowned guest, such figures are in great demand. In uptown New Orleans they are valued like French wines, truffles, or good pâté.

New Orleans being what it is, the string of notables passing through town has been constant, ranging from the future French monarch Louis Philippe (in 1798) to Haile Selassie (in 1950) and Princess Anne (in 1984). Every one of them reported on the warm and bountiful hospitality. The English novelist William Makepeace Thackeray, during his visit in 1856, remarked favorably on a *Medoc* served him at dinner; his host sent him on his way with a case of the stuff. A well-known artist made a similar comment about the mattress in a guest bedroom and his hostess promptly had it delivered to his apartment in New York, *de bon coeur.*

Many prominent figures have returned time and time again. The actress Sarah Bernhardt was so delighted with the way the local Creoles received her that she kept coming back for forty years. On one visit she gave her host a jeweled ring as a house present and received a live alligator in return. Her twenty-two steamer trunks being already packed, she dispatched the beast by separate passage to her home in France. There it proceeded to devour her poodle.

Protocol requires that the prominent guest be received and presented by a civic leader of like stature. For most of the late nineteenth century the mustachioed and dapper former Confederate general, P. G. T. Beauregard, filled this function tirelessly. It was Beauregard who received Oscar Wilde in 1882, obviously without the slightest suspicion regarding the Irish aesthete's looming notoriety.

Heads of state get special treatment. General Charles de Gaulle once came to town to check on his country's former colony and got a boulevard named in his honor. But New Orleans is far more parsimonious than most American cities in handing out place names as party favors. Readers of *Le Monde* clucked over what they mistakenly assumed to be the continuing loyalty of France's former subjects in Louisiana. How could they have known that the "boulevard" in question is a meandering street on the other side of the Mississippi in Algiers? Marshal Foch got the same treatment, but his asphalt monument is out to the north near the shores of Lake Pontchartrain.

The notable visitor to such understated cities as Indianapolis or Portland assumes that he or she has an absolute right to pass judgment on the local scene, like a haughty foreign president reviewing the honor guard sent out to greet him. This sometimes brings out some deliciously condescending behavior at the expense of what is assumed to be the local boobocracy.

One might think that proud New Orleanians would not leave themselves open to this sort of treatment. Yet many people in the Crescent City actually court such condescension by garrulously asking "Well, how do you like New Orleans?" When FDR was in town to dedicate a park, the then mayor, the Honorable Robert Maestri, quizzed him along these lines over lunch at Antoine's, ending his verbal questionnaire with "How do you like dem ersters?"

This touch of provincialism is only half of the picture, however, for New Orleans is at the same time one of those few cities that claim the right to pass judgment on the visiting notable in return. Such judgments are quick, silent, and final. They are disseminated within hours to everyone with the slightest interest in the subject, and they stick for years. Thus, the first sign of big trouble for the Nixon administration was not Watergate but the refusal of Mrs. Nixon and her daughters to bow to Rex, the Lord of Misrule, during their visit to Carnival. In contrast to the Nixon *faux pas*, older folks still recall approvingly how the Duke and Duchess of Windsor executed a flawless *révérence* before Carnival's Royal Highness during their visit.

New Orleans evaluates its visitors severely, but within a somewhat narrow context. The favorable judgment on Oscar Wilde had nothing to do with the volume of poems he had published the year before, but with the details of his deportment while in the Crescent City. Wilde performed his role in the Visiting Dignitary Ritual with grace and aplomb, and was applauded for doing so.

Does this mean that the illustrious visitor must put on the dog to win the approval of New Orleanians? Certainly not. One of the earliest notables to be well received in New Orleans arrived in a miserable state for his brief visit in the 1790's. He was disoriented, filthy, and had a single trunk, but was lauded nonetheless. He was a large grey elephant.

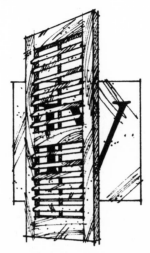

CIVIC SPACE

*In which the distance, actual and perceived,
between New Orleanians is
scientifically calibrated
and found to be short,
even cozy.*

A sense of place

CIVIC SPACE

The Venetian painter Antonio Canaletto (1697-1768) left some wonderful scenes depicting broad Italian piazzas. The air is crystalline and the buildings are meticulously rendered, like an ad for some new 35 mm film. But there is one thing about them that is quite unbelievable to modern American viewers: the large numbers of people just hanging around the piazzas. The places are always teeming with pedestrians. Where are the muggers? The pickpockets? And why weren't those people at work or at home, or at least playing *bocci* ball?

Civic space has been dying a slow death in the United States. Urban crime triggered the downward spiral and the combined forces of television and air-conditioning are finishing the job. People shun public places; they have turned inward.

To some limited extent, Crescent City residents are part of this turn away from civility. It wasn't long ago that windows and doors stood open all over town. Today more and more New Orleanians bar their windows, bolt their doors, and turn on the A/C. Nearly all of them avoid the super-cute, federally-financed (but dangerous) Louis Armstrong Park. (Note the irony: "Satchmo" took up the trumpet at the local Waifs' Home, where he had been sent for packing a pistol.)

The most often cited proof of the declining use of civic space in New Orleans is the fate of stoop-sitting. In the bad old days, the ubiquitous front steps were like Archie Bunker's easy chair—the place you went when you were not working. Not long ago a $13,750 study paid for by you and me via the National Endowment for the Humanities demonstrated that stoop-sitting is all but extinct. Only old-timers still practice the art, claimed the learned sociologists.

As one who has logged several hundred hours a year on a rented stoop, I find reports on the death of stoop-sitting to be premature, thank you. So would my neighbors. Admittedly, few people hose down the front steps these days, but one can still sit in the dirt. Tens of thousands do.

Check for yourself. Wait for a warm evening in late spring and sweep from one end of the town to the other. The stoops are still very much in use. Not only are the stoops in steady use, but thousands of New Orleanians have moved couches out on their front porches in order to survey the passing scene in yet more sybaritic comfort.

Television, air-conditioning, and crime notwithstanding, there are still hordes of New Orleanians who use their civic space. Jackson Square is always mobbed, City Park is tired from use, and the Olmstead-designed paths of Audubon Park are also being worn down by tramping Nikes. Whole sections of North Rampart Street downtown can be packed at 1:00 a.m. on a hot summer's night with pedestrians of all ages, out for a breath of air. The city's park along the shore of Lake Pontchartrain was long a permanent Woodstock until the Levee Board clamped down on the fun.

Why did the sociologists fail to notice this? Maybe because they are glued to their tubes.

PRIVACY

In the northern latitudes, the hearth is home. Even with the advent of central heating, a crackling fire on the hearth still symbolizes that all is well. Which is why a beseiged Richard Nixon closed the windows in the Oval Office, turned up the air-conditioning, and lit a fire in the fireplace.

The symbolism of the hearth is all but meaningless in steamy New Orleans. Far from closing themselves off from the world, the locals for two centuries opened their homes as wide as possible to catch the slightest breath of moving air. The window, not the hearth, brought comfort. This simple reality helped shape New Orleanians' notions of privacy.

As in all Southern cities, New Orleans' historic architecture minimized the distinction between indoors and outdoors, between "my house" and "my street." Humidity also plays a part, for sound waves travel far better in the wet, tropical air of the Deep South than they do in the cool and crisp Northern air. With the windows open wide and the humidity acting as an acoustical amplifier, family arguments in New Orleans became, before air-conditioning, neighborhood affairs.

Far from resenting Nature's invasion of their privacy, New Orleanians readily accepted it. Outdoor galleries on the second floors linked adjoining buildings, and the "double shotgun" frame house was designed as virtually a communal residence.

Back in 1881, New Orleans' finest writer, Lafcadio Hearn, observed that in the double house:

> . . . privacy is impossible; seclusion a mockery.
> Even the attics of two houses open into one another.
> Suppose one is looking for a house and expresses his
> dissatisfaction with this plan, the proprietor will
> exclaim with astonishment: "Why! There is a door
> and the door is closed!"

Hearn's observation was on target. What resident of an older section in New Orleans, lying in bed at night, has not listened in bleary awe to his neighbor's snoring through the paper-thin wall?

"Call in the architects," you say. "Correct the situation!" But think twice before acting. A person's home may be his castle, but try building a community of castles.

NICKNAMES

Here's a little experiment that will enliven your next trip abroad and, if you write up the results, provide a convenient tax deduction to boot. Station yourself on a crowded sidewalk in, say, Tokyo, and photograph the pedestrians. Then, back in your study, measure the average distance among them at rush hour. The shorter the distance, the greater the sense of community. In Tokyo, to continue the example, people tolerate great public closeness. In Los Angeles, by contrast, they demand distance, and build their sidewalks accordingly. It's not just fear of pickpockets, either. In L.A. that other guy is just too "other" for comfort.

Now notice this: in Tokyo people treat one another with great formality, bowing, shaking hands, and exchanging business cards. But in stand-offish L.A., total strangers, when introduced, are immediately on a first-name basis with one another. Even casual acquaintances hug and kiss each other. Once back on the sidewalk, though, those huggers treat one another as muggers.

New Orleanians in public are a cozier people than Angelenos, but they're far behind the Japanese. Up close, however, they are far more likely to use "Mister" or "Missus" than are Californians. Like Southerners generally, they address all Ph.D.'s as "Doctor," the inflection ranging in tone from respectful to derisive.

The threshold of coziness is crossed when the New Orleanian acknowledges that the guy next to him is part of his world, a "we" rather than a "they." Unlike the first person plural in Chicago or Detroit, the New Orleanian's "we" can cross racial, ethnic, or economic lines. It is important simply that the other person have some clear identity in the firmament of the four parishes.

Within the world of "we," intimacy reigns. Men and women who are otherwise total strangers become "hon" and "darling" (pronounced "dawlin"). And if "dawlin" has a nickname, for heaven's sake use it.

New Orleans may well be the nickname capital of the northern hemisphere. Its last two mayors have been "Moon" and "Dutch." No amount of dignity prevents a local Andrew from being "A.J.," an Edward from being "Pud," a William or Henry from being "Bubba," or just about any man "Buddy." That prissy fashion of the 1970's that populated the Northeast with little Geoffreys, Arthurs, Edwards, and Williams ("please don't call our little William 'Billy' ") never reached New Orleans.

"Aha," you say. "This is nothing more than that red-neck polyester usage that led James Earl Carter of Plains, Georgia, to inflict 'Jimmy' on American politics." There is a grain of truth in this charge, but only a grain. For the sheer scale of the nickname industry in New Orleans and Louisiana generally dwarfs even the Georgians' efforts, while the artistry of the product is simply without peer.

Here are a few examples drawn from Louisiana public life today: Larry Napoleon "Boo-ga-loo" Cooper; Milton "Needlenose" Vicknair; Andrew C. "Banana" LeBlanc III; Stanley C. "Lollypop" Bazile; Luke "J-Boy" Guidry; and M. "Chink" Barthe. Most of these nicknames date from the bearers' youth, which suggests that Tom Sawyer-like boyhoods are not yet a thing of the past.

And here are a few samples of the feminine genre. They happen to be drawn from the Junior League's phone list, but they could just as easily have been taken from the ranks of any other club, church, or neighborhood group: Tudie, Mimi, Sparkie, Muffin, BK, Kaki, Teeta, Kink, Kippy, Tippi, Weedie, Bunny, Pixie, Susu, Babs, Bitsie, Cacky (not to be confused with Kaki), Mamsi, Bebe, Lolly, Lulie, Livvy, Ginja, Cheechee, Dee, Ki, Marti, KP, Tibby, Coco, Candy, Rinnie, Suey, Mickey, Skip, Peps, Nita, Bitsy (versus Bitsie), Deanie, Pudney, and Puddin.

English is a cold language. Unlike French or German, it has no intimate form of "you," to be used among friends. The old "thee" and "thou" are used only for the Deity, not for drinking partners. With their nicknames, New Orleanians have tried to fill this gap. It works across generations. You don't want your friends' children to call you by your first name, but "Mr. Marrero" or "Mrs. Schexsnaidre" seems too formal. So you become "Mr. Pud" or Mrs. Banana." By this clever means both community and dignity are preserved.

CLUBS

Who's Who is certainly not designed for New Orleanians. The questionnaire it sends to the eminent leaves plenty of room for them to list their Nobel Prizes, published books, and membership on corporate boards. Significantly, it provides only one scant line for "clubs." To adapt the form for Crescent City usage, the "clubs" category should be followed by at least a half page of blank space.

New Orleans is a club town. Not Diners' Club or Playboy Club, but the real thing—clubby clubs. They exist by the hundreds. There are elite clubs for men or women and not-so-elite clubs for either sex—political clubs, athletic clubs, breakfast clubs, dinner clubs, religious clubs, firemen's clubs, marching clubs, walking clubs, professional clubs, benevolent clubs, joke-telling clubs, bridge clubs, poker clubs. They are called lodges, associations, sodalities, fellowships and even clubs, which is what they all are anyway.

There is scarcely a human activity around which New Orleanians have not organized a club or association. In the old days there were burial clubs, not to mention dozens of other mutual aid societies. Nowadays one can find the Wild Lunch Bunch, the Phunny Phorty Phellows, and the Irish Channel Geographical, Geophysical, Geological, Historical Social Aid and Pleasure Club which meets annually at Parasol's Bar and Restaurant. There is even a flourishing non-club club, the by-laws of which require it to be in a state of permanent recess. The Recess Club meets monthly.

The lion's share of public attention has been accorded the elite clubs. The building of the Boston Club may not compare with that of Boodle's on St. James Street in London or the Pacific Union in San Francisco, but it is handsome nonetheless. And its members are rightfully proud of their venerable institution, the oldest extant men's club in the country. Similarly outranking in protocol all but the New York Yacht Club, the Southern Yacht Club is the proud elder statesman in its league. The latter is not to be confused with the Southern Y'at Club at 526 St. Louis Street, which takes its name not from the nautical group out at the lake, but from the old Mid-City salutation "Wher Y'at?"

The dispensing of prestige is at best a by-product of New Orleans clubs, not their *raison d'être*. Ask a member of the Mecca Benevolent Association why she joined, and she will tell you it was to see friends, have fun, and maybe do some good along the way. You will get the same response from members of the Zulu Social Aid and Pleasure Club. The actual proportions vary from club to club and from member to member, but the basic ingredients are constant: pleasure and service.

In order to maximize both, it is advisable to join not one club but several; four or five is not exceptional, whether among rich or poor, black or white. This number will take care of your social life until you are too old to have one. But don't rule out the further possibility of participating in a couple of quasi-clubs on the side. Just beware. In the same way that galactic clouds have a way of evolving into new nebulae, so informal gatherings at the local bar, tennis court, or pool hall can coalesce into yet more clubs.

What causes this explosion of clubbiness? The very question carries a bias unacceptable to many New Orleanians, who would ask instead why so few clubs exist elsewhere. Yet it is a curious fact that the Creoles of old did not feel the need for clubs beyond a handful of masonic lodges and a few other church related groups. It was the Anglo-Saxon newcomers who were addicted to them. Through their clubs, these unwelcome immigrants from the North attained a degree of stability in a society they found alien, confusing, and in the early days, well beyond their control. From the Anglo-Saxon immigrants the ideal of clubbiness spread quickly among other ethnic groups, the members of which handily mastered the art of association building.

And build they did. Even the Creoles' informal revelries at the time of Mardi Gras were taken over and reorganized into clubs or "krewes." Clubs begat clubs with Malthusian swiftness, and the process continues to this day. Thus, the Jugs Social and Pleasure Club in 1970 formed the "NOMTOC (JUGS)," which tries to live up to its name as "New Orleans' Most Talked Of Club." At carnival time it is the terror of Algiers.

The name of the NOMTOC group implies that it is no easy matter to become the most talked about club in the Crescent City. Actually, the reverse is true. It's a cinch, for most of the clubs are not talked about at all and prefer not to be. This laudable trait, so rare in a world of institutional self-promotion, requires a correction in our initial observation about *Who's Who*. Since New Orleans clubs would not wish their members to list them, *Who's Who* can leave its questionnaire as it is.

NEIGHBORHOODS

Until recent decades, October 1st marked a most important moment in the New Orleans year—Rent Day. It was then that all leases were ended or renewed. The streets would be full of wagons and trucks of families on the move. The tradition of

Rent Day has died out, but New Orleanians are still urbanized gypsies. Strange to say, though, New Orleanians rarely move more than a few blocks. And so, for all the mobility of its native-born population, New Orleans remains a city of neighborhoods.

From the Irish Channel to Faubourg Treme, each neighborhood of the Crescent City has its own distinctive character. Some can be recognized by the shade of their natives' accent, or by the songs children chant on school playgrounds. Many neighborhood peculiarities are rooted in the life of a particular church or parish, local bar or corner grocery. The latter is a French legacy, for the Creoles encouraged the establishment of shops on each corner, to serve the households in between. Such shops often maintained the only telephone on the block. Everyone met there, and in some neighborhoods people still do. Corner stores foster a sense of community and are surely one of the factors contributing to the low level of vandalism which, according to Dr. Ralph Thayer of the University of New Orleans, distinguishes the Crescent City from other American megalopolae.

It is inconceivable that this neighborhood life would not seep into politics. In fact, New Orleans politics are to a considerable degree the politics of neighborhoods. They have been so ever since Canal Street separated the French Quarter from the Anglo-Saxons' Faubourg St. Mary. Significantly, median strips in New Orleans are still called "neutral grounds," which is better than "No Man's Land" or "DMZ" but nonetheless conjures up the image of an armed border region.

Many of the most potent political forces in the Crescent City have grown from specific neighborhoods. The Seventh Ward Civic Association is no longer what it once was, but in its heyday a generation ago, Lou "Napoleon" Scanlon, its boss, commanded four hundred members and had more patronage than an Ottoman pasha. Seventh Ward picnics were as famous for their political deals as for their jambalaya, beer, and jazz.

Many forces are eroding neighborhood life today. Supermarkets and blandly impersonal drugstore chains replace corner shops. Urban renewal, gentrification, television and upward mobility are shaking up neighborhoods more than Rent Day ever did.

But don't give up on those corners of local life too quickly. Claiborne Avenue used to run its stately tree-lined course through the heart of an ancient and heavily black district. Then the Federal Highway Administration teamed up with local philistines to drive a six-lane viaduct down the center. The neighborhood began to crumble and all the signs of decay appeared: burnt-out buildings, drugs, and crime. Social service agencies struck out on Claiborne Avenue. Today, however, a new neighborhood organization is bringing fresh life to the area. The Tamborine and Fan Club combats crime and drugs. It is also reviving the colorful festivals at Carnival time—all in the grim shadow of that unwelcomed viaduct.

Amputees frequently report experiencing strong sensations in their nonexistent arm or leg. A phenomenon like this seems to be occurring on Claiborne Avenue. But there the sensations are harbingers of genuine renewal.

NEIGHBORS

New Orleans has had its share of racial tension, which is not surprising for the place where slaves were "sold down the river." A legacy of segregated schools, shops, and transportation is just part of the problem. Fully a century ago Lafcadio Hearn wrote a chilling tale about police brutality against blacks.

But there is another side to the story. Before Emancipation, New Orleans had by far the largest population of "free persons of color" of any city in North America. And after the Civil War, Jim Crow segregation was slow in coming to town. Black and white baseball teams played exhibition games against each other throughout the 1880's, and black and white jockeys and boxers competed together down to the early 1890's. Full segregation of streetcars did not come until 1902, and the worst laws discriminating against blacks as voters are of the same vintage. The era of complete segregation spans the memory of only one generation.

Backwardness has its virtues. New Orleans lagged far behind many cities in introducing zoning laws. Until 1929, in fact, you were free to build anything anywhere, and people did. Fine homes, barrooms, shotgun dwellings for the poor, and corner groceries were all mixed together, often in the same block. So were black and white families. A few local cynics argue that this pattern of housing was due solely to the fact that rich whites wanted their black servants to live nearby. But this does not explain why the same racial commingling in housing extended to neighborhoods where everyone was poor. It does not explain why the pioneer black jazzman, Buddy Bolden of First Street, lived two doors from the family of Larry Shields, the white clarinetist with the Original Dixieland Jazz Band. Nor does it account for the poor but fully integrated neighborhood around Frenchman and Robertson Streets in Faubourg Marigny in which Ferdinand "Jelly Roll" Morton grew up.

Perhaps it was the Latin and Catholic atmosphere. Visit any Anglo-Saxon Episcopal church in Virginia and notice the seating. The architects saw to it that the races communicated separately with God. In Creole New Orleans things were different, as the English tourist Harriet Martineau observed in 1837:

> Then there is the Cathedral to be attended, a place which the
> European gladly visits, as the only one in the United States where
> all men meet together as brethren...Within the edifice there is no
> separation...kneeling on the pavement may be seen a multitude of
> every shade of complexion, from the fair Scotchwoman or German,
> to the jet-black, pure African.

New Orleans today, no less than Philadelphia or Minneapolis, is full of all-white and all-black organizations. There are also a few 100 percent color-coded neighborhoods, which were a great rarity in the past. And there are some resentments on both sides that have been nurtured for decades and flare up at any provocation, large or small. But there are some prominent citizens of both races who have dedicated their lives to maintaining harmony within the biracial community, people who take action because they know it is the right thing to do, and because both they and the city will gain from it.

THE BRICKS

Lafitte, Iberville, St. Thomas, St. Bernard, Desire—all names that are redolent with the spirit of Old New Orleans. They are also names of housing projects built with Federal Housing Authority money in the decades after 1939. Solidly constructed and intended as model housing for the middle class, they were the pride of New Orleans' Mayor Morrison. Today they are frightful slums inhabited almost entirely by poor blacks. Outsiders of all races, especially police officers, fear to enter them. As if to set them off from New Orleans' traditional wooden housing stock, they are known as "The Bricks."

"The Bricks" are not happy places either for visitors or residents. They are federally planned ghettos within a traditionally unghettoized city. They are wracked with drugs and violent crime.

Here are some statistics. 15,708 adults reside in "The Bricks," along with 30,083 minors. There are only 1,271 two-parent families living in "The Bricks" and only 4,818 people whom the Housing Authority of New Orleans classifies as "workers." Stated differently, there are two minors for every adult, twenty-five children for every two-parent family, and six unemployed minors for every gainfully employed worker.

So much for statistics. "The Bricks" are also home to many church elders, teenagers who worry about their math exam on Friday, and anxious mothers who sew for their children and scrub them up for visits to Aunt Carol over on Dryades Street. Don't forget the schoolteachers either, or actress Frosine Thomas, singers Charles and Aaron Neville, or Benny Jones, who pounds the bass drum for the exciting new Dirty Dozen Brass Band. They all look on "The Bricks" as home.

CUTTHROATS

I t is no secret that New Orleans has its share of crime. From time to time the Mayor, his eye cocked on the tourist industry, tries to sweep aside all the murder and theft by claiming either that more crimes are reported now, or, police record-keeping has improved. Meanwhile, violent crime continues to insinuate itself into people's daily lives. No neighborhood or group is spared.

In the Sixth District crime is a minute-by-minute reality. Besides embracing four federally built housing projects (New Orleans' only true ghettos), the Sixth includes the posh Garden District. In a typical six-month span, the 67,000 residents of the Sixth District experienced 1,500 disturbances, 400 armed robberies, and five times the rate of murder and rape of any other region of the city. Cops at the local station house call the district Fort Apache.

It is hard to explain to a tourist who has been mugged that crime visits New Orleans less frequently than it does many major American cities. But the statistics confirm it and reveal, furthermore, that the situation is improving. In light of the fact that crime in New Orleans is on the wane, it is the more regrettable that so many people there are prepared to accept an increasingly brutalized world as inevitable. Yet they do, and the local press is not above pandering to their mood. As a result, the sense of community that manifests itself so strikingly at times exists in constant tension with a sense of fear.

Events sometimes occur that seem to justify the worst possible suspicions of one's neighbor. Not long ago the police discovered that a Chicago man (he had to be from "up there somewhere") was storing fifty pounds of fresh meat in the refrigerator of his apartment at 2619 North Robertson Street. Sharp-eyed investigators quickly learned that most of the neighbors' dogs were missing. A fiend was loose in Orleans Parish, and soon the whole town was buzzing.

But there was worse to come. After examining several hunks of the meat, the coroner, Dr. Minyard (a jazz trumpeter in his spare time) announced decisively that "I think definitely that this is human flesh, and there has definitely been a murder here." No sooner was the good doctor's pronouncement in print than everyone began to ask the obvious question: what was the Chicagoan doing with all those cutlets of neighbor? The grisly answer came with the discovery on the kitchen table of several bags of seasoning; not good Creole spices either, but strange Oriental seasonings.

For weeks the city savored the lurid details. The newspaper reported "a face pressed against a window...a low voice murmuring late at night." And everyone was reminded just how frail is the web of civility that enables us all to live together.

MODEL CITIES

In the bygone days of Lyndon Johnson, the federal government devised a Model Cities program. Selected communities across the country were to be turned into earthly paradises, laboratory models of how we will all live some day. But the program died and so did many of its Model Cities.

From the eighteenth century to the present New Orleans has had its own Model Cities program. Unlike LBJ's, however, this one was designed to be dead from the outset and has turned out to be a glittering success. The cemeteries of the Crescent City are, as Mark Twain noted, gleaming "Cities of the Dead." And very impressive ones at that. "If those people down there would live as neatly while they were alive as they do after they are dead," wrote Mark Twain, "they would find many advantages to it."

New Orleans' cemeteries have always embodied ideals of housing and town planning that are more advanced than those practiced by the living natives. When the Creoles were still dwelling in boxy little houses, they were making plans to spend eternity in elegant Greek temples. And when the more conformist Anglo-Saxons took to living in monotonous rows of temples, they dared to erect Italian villas and fanciful gothic structures for their postmortem days. In her townhouse before the turn of the century, Mrs. John Dibert adhered slavishly to all the conventions of the day. But for her tomb she hired an interior decorator and urged him to give free reign to his imagination.

The planning ideals of this necropolis have not always warranted applause. While alive, New Orleans' wealthy citizens always accepted the reality of poorer neighbors coexisting with them in the same neighborhoods. But scarcely had Metairie Cemetery opened its gates than Millionaire's Row appeared, an exclusive enclave for the departed rich.

Blockbusting is all but impossible when the older residents are no longer able to move out. The only recorded case of blockbusting among the dead occurred when a former king of Zulu, the black carnival krewe, was interred in the abandoned Girod Street Cemetery, run by the Episcopal Church. Some of the corpses apparently complained, and so vehemently that the entire cemetery was sold to make room for the Superdome the moment the offer was made.

The twentieth-century subdivision, planned as a single and utterly standardized unit, made its New Orleans debut with the Catholic Archdiocese's Levitowns for the dead. Mass production brought the price of a marble edifice within the reach of the man in the street. And if the streets themselves had grown dangerous, the mortuary subdivisions were safe, even bucolic.

This form of collective security was gained at a price. The planners required that all vaults be nearly identical. Individual owners can modify the trimmings but not the basic design. "It's pretty much the same principle as in real estate," observes Mr. Frank Rome, Executive Director of Cemeteries for the Archdiocese. Predictably, the new marble suburbias are still suburbias.

It remained for the city government to open the last frontier in mortuary properties: rental units. In the old days the city sold plots, but no more. Now the city retains title and the possibility of reusing the same vault later. This is pretty grim stuff if you anticipate a long stay in eternity. But there are advantages. Whereas the living must haggle with corrupt landlords and hustling real estate agents, the dead can rest in the assurance that they have been treated honestly and fairly. Indeed, the city guarantees the exclusion of tomb scalpers from its marble Model Cities.

The next frontier in sepulchral real estate is bound to be time sharing. When this comes to pass, a couple in Syracuse can arrange to have their mortal remains spend part of each year in the Carrollton Cemetery in New Orleans, and part in, say, Greenwood Cemetery in Brooklyn, Forest Lawn in Los Angeles, or even Père Lachaise in Paris. Life, as they say, is never dull for a moment.

DEATH

*In which a macabre subject is
introduced and found to be, in
New Orleans at least, almost
Jolly!*

At rest above the water table

64

DEATH

Genealogy is hot stuff in New Orleans. If genealogical researchers were to extend their inquiry beyond the human family, however, they would quickly discover that the prize of ancient lineage in The Crescent City would have to go to *aedes aegypti,* the urban mosquito. This pioneer settler arrived on the shores of the Mississippi with the first *Homo sapiens,* and its progeny thrived there until our own century. Only the collateral lines of the family continue today, but at its height the mosquito clan took on the entire human community and nearly won. Its weapon was yellow fever, "Yellow Jack" in local lore. New Orleanians by the thousands perished in yellow fever epidemics. Indeed, yellow fever made its last stand in North America in New Orleans as late as 1905.

The statistics are staggering. Yellow fever and cholera devastated the city in 1832-33, sending more than five thousand citizens to their deaths. The first traffic jam in New Orleans occurred as wagons of corpses lined up at the cemeteries. In 1866 another thousand citizens died of cholera, and in 1878 *aedes aegypti* killed off almost four thousand more. The deadly mosquito's final assault on New Orleans dispatched half a thousand more people to their graves, and stories of the gruesome deaths are still a part of the living memory of many New Orleans families and neighborhoods.

Between these major epidemics, the city was punished by constant fluxes, fevers, and consumption, not to mention smallpox and leprosy, the latter being the subject of a particularly macabre story, "Jean-ah Poquelin," in George Washington Cable's *Old Creole Days.* The only leper hospital on the continent was founded and still exists on an old plantation up-river from the city.

The epidemics are safely in the past, of course. But they left their mark everywhere. New Orleans' cultural life was created by survivors, by people haunted by death. Perhaps more than other American communities, New Orleans lived in dread of it.

Frequent epidemics and constant pestilence meant that death in New Orleans was not merely a private drama occuring in the intimate circle of one's family, but a civic event, experienced by the entire community. Understandably, the survivors' mourning, as well as their efforts to escape from death's presence and to compensate for it through giddy revelry, took place in public. And in surprising ways.

DANCING

Each week the *Metroplex Want Ads* appear in Orleans and neighboring parishes. Its "Lonely Hearts" announcements cover a full page, between household effects and used cars. These four-line ads are like notes in bottles tossed out on the civic waves. In these, the lonely specify all the interests they are seeking in The Perfect Mate. A careful statistical examination of the qualities specified in the ads over many months reveals a most curious phenomenon. The preferred inclinations include walking, travelling, sports, watching TV, and just plain relaxing. But heading the list, way out in front of everything else, are dancing and dining.

No local would be surprised by this. As early as 1743, a French officer wrote the folks back home that New Orleanians spent all their money on balls and feasting. When Jefferson bought Louisiana, the first problem that the new American government faced was to convince New Orleanians that their public balls would not be discontinued. And one of the first fights under the new regime broke out over the question of whether French or American dances would lead off the weekly assemblies.

Some eighty establishments offered public balls in the nineteenth century. French Creoles danced; Anglo-Saxons danced; Blacks danced; new immigrants danced; Creoles of Color danced; everyone danced. They still do, except on Bourbon Street, where "they" are not the locals.

Even when the city is smothered by summer heat and when the humidity is at levels that would produce a downpour anywhere else, the sweaty revelers at Munster's Dance Hall uptown on Laurel Street are jumping and gyrating. Last Saturday, many of the same people who danced at the New Orleans Country Club at a midday party showed up at the Art Museum's ball for four more hours of hoofing at night. Stella Scott, born on a plantation near St. Martinville and now a resident on Bienville Street, loves nothing better than to dine in the Quarter on Saturday night, have several martinis, and then dance to street troubadours. Mrs. Scott is 93.

Strange to say, all this frivolity occurs in the very city which, for over two centuries, Death visited more ruthlessly than anywhere else on the continent. Maybe Sigmund Freud was right when he wrote:

> The experience of satisfaction is connected with the initial helplessness (**Hilfslosigkeit**) of human beings.
>
> ...Sigmund Freud,
> *Projects for a Scientific Psychology*

DRESS CODE

"Clothes make the man," it is said, but the reverse is nearer to the truth. The shape of society is reflected in the clothing people wear.

Up to our own century, for example, it was possible to discover a person's profession or the region of the country he came from simply by examining his or her clothing. Such an inspection would also reveal that person's standing in the great pecking order of society.

Now all this has changed. Farmers wear Dior suits and their wives carry Gucci bags. Stockbrokers sport Levi's, while salesgirls invest in Ungaro dresses. It's all very confusing, but then so is life.

Until recently, New Orleans' steamy summers defined local dress, which consisted of washable cottons for men and women alike. The hometown firm of Haspel provided loosely-cut washable suits for men at such low prices that even a junior clerk could afford a closet full. Even today, twenty years after the advent of air conditioning, the comfortable, rumpled look is still favored by many older and more proper New Orleans males. To be sure, there are the blow-dried young, with huge class rings on their fingers and tasseled loafers of soft leather on their feet, silky sleek fellows who wear three-piece suits the year round. But they are viewed— correctly—as *Auslaenders,* Texans in spirit if not genealogy. As to women, in the bad old days they were expected to sit out the hottest hours of the day at home under the ceiling fan.

Now that almost all buildings are air-conditioned, any remaining distinctive aspects of local dress can be attributed solely to the tenacity of custom rather than to climate. There are not many such distinctions left, but two are striking.

First, New Orleans clothing stores concentrate heavily on the fancy and the very inexpensive, with rather little for those whose tastes and resources are in between. This is especially noticeable in women's wear. With more affluent New Orleans females filling traditional roles than grubbing away in the labor force, local shops offer a relatively greater selection in satin pumps than in the practical business shoes that fill the shop windows in Washington, D.C. The "Big Easy" is no middle-class town.

The chief buyer at Brooks Brothers' shop on Canal Street reports the second difference: "We sell more formal wear here than in any other city, and more tails than in New York and Washington combined." New Orleanians purchase such garb for dancing and partying. Even people of modest means indulge their passion for fancy dress, for it is deemed essential for good partying, which in turn is felt to be essential for survival.

Women's shops present the same picture. Gloria Steinem might have to look hard to find a charcoal grey business suit in the Crescent City, but she would have an awesome array of designer gowns from which to choose. And by no means are all the buyers of such wares affluent.

Harriet Martineau observed during her travels in 1835 that "New Orleans is the only place in the United States where I am aware of seeing a particle of rouge." The rouge is still in evidence, and it is backed up by several fine local *parfumeurs,* not to mention New Orleans' court jeweler, Mignon Faget.

Social historians and students of marketing might ponder the fact that Ms. Faget advertises her gold and silver creations on the side of New Orleans' streetcars. It is doubtful that Tiffany's ever found it advantageous to plug its goods on New York buses, not even on the Fifth Avenue line. But then again, do New Yorkers have anything in their collective memory so grim as the deadly epidemics of New Orleans? Lacking that, New Yorkers can afford to be grave and serious. New Orleanians cannot.

E L E G Y

Open the New Orleans paper on any day. There, between the classifieds and the obituaries, is a column or more of snapshots. They show both men and women, white and black. Most of the subjects are young and many are smiling, as if for a picture to be given to grandparents or in-laws, or perhaps to be printed in the school yearbook. But all of the subjects are dead, and these are "Memorials."

Such memorials are not cheap. To print the picture alone costs $48.75, which reserves a twenty-five line space. But that is not all. Beneath each picture is a poem of four to fifteen lines, which runs another ten or fifteen dollars to print.

Reading them, one might think that the poems all came from one and the same hand, namely the author of the Burma Shave signs of yore. Here is a sample:

> You left us—oh! You left us,
> In this sad vale of tears;
> We miss you! Oh! We miss you
> Through all the dreary years...

The hypothesis about single authorship is not far off the mark. At no cost, *The*

Times-Picayune's Classified Department provides the nonpoetic bereaved with a silver-bound volume of memorial verses from which to choose. Without delving into the reasons for which the Classified Department rather than the Obituary Department assumes this responsibility, let us simply note that the volume is extremely convenient for the consumer. One can order any of the two hundred and twenty-three selections by number, the verse quoted being No. 153. Many have blanks where the name of the loved one can be inserted. Some provide instructions on how to modify the text in order to preserve the meter in the face of multisyllabic names like Albertine, Florian, or Ofilio.

Which poems do New Orleanians select? Not surprisingly, they spurn those that are clearly alien imports. Not once in three years, for example, has anyone taken No. 54, which speaks of "your cold and lonely grave"; New Orleanians, after all, have traditionally buried their dead not in graves but in tombs, which are never very cold and, due to crowding, rarely lonely.

The favorites by far are those that affirm a Christian afterlife and that hold out the chance of a future reunion with the lost one. Anyone claiming that we live in a secular society would do well to ponder this. And the reunion in the beyond is rarely conceived as a private affair. The whole family will be there, and often friends and neighbors as well. Evidently, there are front stoops in Heaven, too.

Anthropologists have spoken wisely of the need to mourn, not privately but collectively. Jessica Mitford and others have regretted Americans' attempts to individualize and privatize death. But tens of thousands of New Orleanians have so far avoided this aspect of twentieth-century life. They hold public wakes and public funerals. They mourn together and use the newspaper to invite the whole world to join them.

And some don't even rely on that silver book of memorial poems. With apologies to no English teacher, they pen their own versified messages to the dead, which are then conveniently delivered by *The Times-Picayune*. Most are doggerel, but even the worst are genuine folk art. And every month or so the "Memorials" contain an original poem that is moving in its directness and beauty. Then even casual readers, like me, are drawn into sharing a stranger's grief.

ALL SAINTS DAY

Since the time of Pope Gregory III (731-741 A.D.), November 1st has been dedicated to the memory of all saints and martyrs of the Church. In Europe, the tombs of thousands of local saints are cleaned up and decorated on this day. In an uncharacteristic surge of tidiness, people in the Mediterranean world extend the clean-up to other graves nearby, especially those of their own families. This practice came to New Orleans with the French.

On All Saints Day New Orleans cemeteries are filled with people working. They whitewash the tombs and place chrysanthemums, real or plastic, on the graves or on nearby hillocks of sand and shell. Styrofoam crosses, wicker baskets, and both real and artificial roses are sold in the shops. It is truly *"Le jour des morts,"* a kind of Mardi Gras for the dead.

There have been reports for a century that the practice of celebrating All Saints Day is on the wane. This may be. At the very least, by the middle of our century some of the cemeteries had become so unsafe as to scare away even the most devoted families of the dead. Finally, public-spirited citizens in the early 1980's banded together to assure safe access to the most ancient downtown cemeteries. Police were posted at the gates and people felt safe once more. The observation of All Saints Day revived.

On All Saints Day just last year at the grand old Saint Louis Cemetery No. 2, in which stand the tombs of many distinguished black Creole families, the bustle of work proceeded until sunset, as if making up for lost time. Members of the Barbarin family, prominent in band music since the 1880's, brought their instruments with them to the cemetery. Once they finished cleaning and whitewashing the tomb, three generations of Barbarins took their horns from their cases and played a musical tribute to their ancestral past. Nearby, other families quietly went about their business.

NATURE'S CAPRICE

*In which it is shown how Mother Nature's
capriciousness leaves folks in south Louisiana
eager to gamble on a better future,
or just to gamble.*

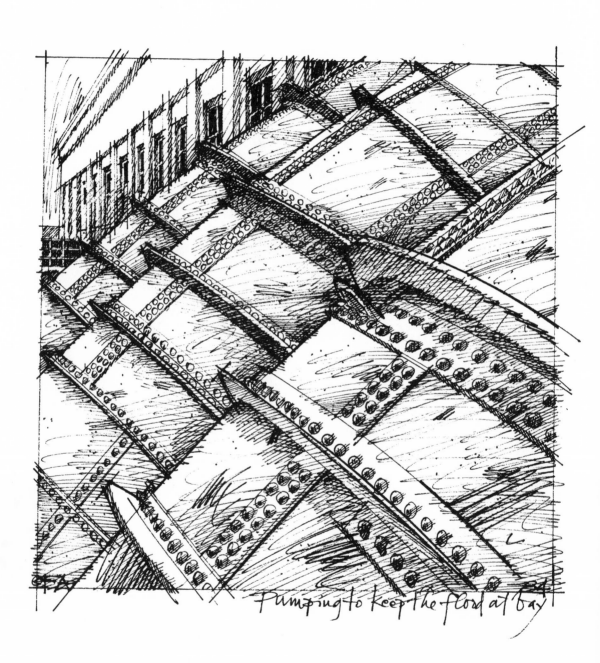

Pumping to keep the flood at bay

NATURE'S CAPRICE

Nature in New Orleans can be gentle, bounteous, and infinitely seductive in her charms. But she can also throw tantrums, and has done so with unnerving frequency over the centuries.

She has wiped out entire city blocks through fire, dispatched thousands to their graves through disease, and permanently washed away whole districts through flooding. Just a decade ago, dense black clouds of mosquitoes descended on the rural parishes north of the Crescent City, suffocating the hordes of livestock that could not avoid inhaling them.

No San Andreas fault underlies Orleans Parish, but the threat of natural disaster is no less omnipresent there than in San Francisco. A marine geologist at Louisiana State University has studied the Gulf of Mexico's steady erosion of neighboring Plaquemines Parish and predicts the complete disappearance beneath the waves of the former stronghold of the Perez family within fifty-two years. In two thousand years the site of New Orleans itself will be gone.

A more immediate doomsday scenario will be played out whenever the Mississippi decides to carve into the levee above Baton Rouge. When that happens, the mighty river will shift its course and charge headlong to the Gulf through what is now the Atchafalaya Basin, west of New Orleans. This shift will leave the Crescent City in the lurch, marooned on an aquatic blind alley formed by the blocked channel of the Mississippi.

Even more immediate is the threat of hurricanes, for New Orleans lies directly on their most heavily frequented line of march. As everyone knows locally, a hurricane can be horrible. If a bad one hits, the anti-hurricane gear sold at Harry's Hardware on Magazine Street will be useless. When hurricane Camille crashed onto the nearby Gulf Coast in 1969, the tidal waves washed heavy modern coffins out of the ground, just in time for low barometric pressure to pop them open and hurl the corpses into the tree tops. Scores of houses were swept away as well, leaving only the stoops remaining. This occured at Pass Christian, Mississippi—New Orleanians' most favored seaside spa.

Heroic efforts are being made to avert a similar disaster in New Orleans. The city's levees along Lake Pontchartrain are being raised to discourage some future hurricane from driving the shallow waters of the lake into downtown New Orleans. But no one who watched roofs being ripped off and mighty oaks uprooted when Hurricane Betsy hit New Orleans in 1965 thinks that such measures can do more than limit the damage. In the end, the city's fate is in the hands of powers it cannot control. Small wonder, then, that a note of fatalism runs through New Orleans' entire history down to the present.

Ignatius J. Reilly of Constantinople Street, the philosophical hero of John Kennedy Toole's *Confederacy of Dunces,* understood this well. A disciple of Anicius Manilus Severinus Boethius (480-524 A.D.), Reilly quotes his ancient mentor to show that fate—Fortuna —rules in human affairs, and that all striving is ultimately meaningless. His solution? "When Fortuna spins you downward, go to a movie and get more out of life." In other words, adopt a pleasure-seeking state of resignation. That, presumably, is the reason many people in the Gulf Coast neighborhoods threatened by Camille decided to devote their last hours to partying before the cataclysm hit. A few of these good folk even survived.

WATER

Amidst all the frivolity, don't make the mistake of thinking that New Orleanians take nothing seriously. They do, and like ancient Greeks, they begin with fundamentals: earth, air, fire and water.

Actually, earth can be dismissed, since in New Orleans it is largely mixed with, and frequently submerged under, water. Air can be dismissed as well, since for half of the year the local climate is a kind of soggy noncombusting fire. That leaves fire and water as the elements to be taken most seriously.

Fire is a constant threat in what remains largely a wooden city. Twice, in 1788 and 1794, the central district of the city went up in smoke. Even today, neighborhood life is frequently punctuated by the roar of sirens and the acrid smell of burnt wood. Conflagrations were so commonplace in the nineteenth century that a veritable army of volunteer fire departments was formed. These were such important organizations that they became pioneers in the social service field, providing members with everything from family insurance to funerals with bands.

It is water that is most feared. First, there are the Mississippi River and Lake Pontchartrain, both of which are held back by high earthen levees. These are the Levee Board's domain, and one doesn't joke about the Levee Board. The stakes are too high.

Then there is rain, constant rain, some sixty-two inches of it each year: high by any standard. For some inexplicable climatological reason, the posh Garden District is deluged with several additional inches annually, suggesting that divine justice never rests.

Since the city lies beneath sea level, every drop of this rain water must be pumped up and out. So must sewage, but through a separate system. General Ulysses S. Grant observed that Venice would be a nice place if the inhabitants would drain the streets. New Orleans has four times the number of canals and covered culverts as Venice. And there is a series of somber brick pumping stations, where huge locally-designed screw pumps palpitate night and day. Holland now uses similar machines designed after the New Orleans prototypes.

This vast domain is controlled by the thirteen members of the Sewerage and Water Board. These gentlemen—recently joined by one gentlewoman—are taken seriously, not only by their 1500 employees, by their spouses, and by themselves, but by the public at large. And well they might be. They serve for twelve years, as against the mayor's four. Mayors give speeches, but the Sewerage and Water Board is the only thing standing between New Orleans and Atlantis.

A tug of war with nature has gone on since 1718. In the earlier years of this century nature lost ground fast, thanks to the installation of a new city-wide drainage system. Gradually nature bounced back, and for an unexpected reason. When the drainage system was planned in the 1890's, it was assumed that eighty-five percent of all rain would be absorbed into the ground. With the spread of pavement and construction, only twenty percent is now absorbed. The pumping capacity of 6,600 cubic feet per minute is impressive, but a 10,000 cubic foot capacity is called for right away, or else we'll need an ark. Insurance companies appreciate the danger. Flood insurance would be more expensive in New Orleans than in any other major city were it not for federal assistance.

A shower of only one or two inches causes little notice in soggy New Orleans. With the first warnings of a more serious downpour, however, the city braces itself. Prized furniture is moved upstairs and rugs are rolled up. Since the streets are several inches lower than the neutral grounds and curbs, cars are parked on the grassy center strips, looking for all the world like turtles clustered on a patch of high ground in a swamp.

Such precautions are often inadequate. Twice in the last decade rowboats have plied the streets of uptown New Orleans. The last time a major flood hit town, a member of the Sewerage and Water Board was discovered at the helm of one such craft, in the street before his home, looking like a Venetian gondolier. Polite people did not laugh, nor did the others. For not everything that is funny is laughable.

SNOW

Every decade or so, a few flurries of snow fall on New Orleans. Otherwise, snow is something New Orleans kids see on television or try to conjure up from Santa Claus stories. Unless New Orleanians travel, their only contact with this white substance is through the handiwork of Mr. George J. Ortolano, founder (in 1943) of the Sno Wizard Manufacturing Company at 3436 Magazine Street.

Ortolano invented the Sno Wizard, a $1,200 cast iron grinder that produces shaven ice "comparable to Mother Nature's fine, fluffy snow," to quote the sales brochure. No New Orleans neighborhood is without a Sno Wizard, which is usually installed in the doorway of a wooden shed or in a corner grocery.

For a mere twenty-five cents the proprietor unleashes the Sno Wizard's tri-cutter steel blades, which revolve at 1,725 rpm to shave huge blocks of ice into fine snow. This is then packed into cones, over which is poured an infinite variety of colored syrups with flavors like anisette, coconut, lime, strawberry and watermelon. The rows of clear bottles, unlabeled, glisten in the sunlight like fine old wine. Small children stand on tiptoe as they lean over the half door from the sidewalk to place their orders and select their favorite syrups.

New Orleans snoballs: so simple, yet to this simpler world, as exotic as the spices Marco Polo brought back from Cathay.

Juridical postscript: Mr. Tyrone Jack of 1110 B Newton Street in New Orleans robbed a snoball stand of $32.90 at gunpoint, departing the scene. After a short chase on bicycle and then on foot, Jack was captured by a Jefferson Parish patrolman. In spite of a spirited defense by his attorney, Tyrone Jack was given a prison sentence of ninety-nine years, which was raised to a total of 198 years when he was linked with another unsolved crime. In New Orleans, one should not mess with the snoball industry.

CRAPS

Who are the gamblers among your friends? Whatever their other traits of character, they probably would all agree that blind luck plays a big role in human affairs. What, then, should one make of a city that has harbored more gamblers and more games of chance than any other city in North America, including Las Vegas?

As early as the 1830's there was a gambling house on Orleans Street that was open twenty-four hours a day, seven days a week. By the time of the Civil War the city claimed hundreds of houses employing an estimated four thousand dealers, cappers and croupiers. The numbers grew thereafter, and continued to grow down to our own century.

Gambling in America, real gambling, is inseparably linked with the Crescent City. Everyone knows the jazz tune, "Tiger Rag," which began life as a New Orleans quadrille. Less well known is the fact that its name is derived from the card game of Faro, which is similar to black jack and known in New Orleans as "The Tiger." To gamble at Faro was "to buck the tiger." The term was also used in New Orleans barrelhouse lingo for the lowest hand you could draw in a poker game. It took nerves of steel to "hold the tiger."

Similarly, everyone knows that in baseball a home run with the bases loaded is a "grand slam." This phrase came originally from another game of chance called "Boston"—this one invented by British officers during the siege of Boston and soon thereafter imported to New Orleans. The proudest and most ancient men's club in New Orleans today is the Boston Club, founded in 1841 to court the "grand slam."

The ultimate game of chance was and is crap shooting, which also bears the seal of New Orleans. A game similar to craps was being played in Paris at the time of the French Revolution. Visitors from New Orleans discovered it there and brought it back with them to wow the good ol' boys on Rue Royale. Americans in the Crescent City were fascinated by the new game, which they associated with the town's French playboys. The Americans' slang name for the Creole frenchman was "Johnny Crapoud," or "Johnny the Frog." The "Crapauds' " game soon became known as "craps."

Faro, Boston, and craps are fine games for betting but they have one disadvantage: They are not good in large groups, and in a real gambling town scale eventually becomes important. Bingo has obvious advantages, and vast halls in nearby Jefferson Parish are regularly turned over to it, *ad majoram Dei gloriam.* But bingo is dull, terminally dull, except to the folks who play it.

There are only two other ways to engage large numbers of people in gambling; horse racing and the lottery. New Orleans loves the horses; back before the Civil

War the track in nearby Metairie was the capital of American turf racing. Today the local fairgrounds has the honor of being one of the few places in America where races are run on Sunday.

Unfortunately, most of the fun in horse racing is in being out at the track. Not so for the lottery, which you can enjoy from your living room or the corner bar. And lottery lends itself to prodigious scale. Indeed, the nearest America ever came to a national lottery was the annual five hundred million dollar New Orleans-based monster known as the "Louisiana Lottery." Until the U.S. Congress finally killed it in 1890, this lottery was so big and so lucrative to its sponsors that it didn't have to be rigged. After turning half the country into gamblers, the Louisiana Lottery finally faded, but a variant lived on in the game of keno, which even in the 1940's employed a thousand people in the Crescent City. Everyone played.

New Orleanians' addiction to games of chance was strengthened by many factors, not the least of which was the fact that so few puritans ever found their way to City Hall. City fathers, ever the realists, recognized the local propensity for gambling and took advantage of it. New Orleans' first municipal revenue came from a tax on billiard tables and taverns. That was in 1770 under the Spanish. Two years after the Americans took over in 1803, a new College of Orleans was created and financed— by a lottery. Charity Hospital, still the city's largest, grew rapidly on the proceeds from the Louisiana Lottery.

Today public gambling is outlawed in New Orleans. It thrives on, however. Police claim that two million dollars in bets are placed with local bookmakers each week during the football season. This is illegal, of course, but *The Times-Picayune* conveniently advises its readers which teams have the best odds.

Even though private gambling is alive, well, and virtually public, the Crescent City has nonetheless lost its preeminent position in the world of chance. Since it is obvious that New Orleanians today are no less entranced than in the past by the power of blind luck in human affairs, this must indicate that the rest of America is finally catching up with Johnny Crapaud's old town.

FUND-RAISER

Musicians in New Orleans have always had to hustle for a living. A nineteenth-century bassoonist named Passage kept body and soul together by doubling as a fencing master on the side. At one performance in 1814 he first played a bassoon solo and then, after the intermission, dueled in an exhibition match with another master fencer—which is perhaps the source of the jazz term "cutting contest." Today's symphony musicians in New Orleans follow sidelines ranging from auto mechanic to restaurant chef.

Touched with pity for these poor fellows, the local public has often mounted benefits especially to help the musicians. When an overly enthusiastic violinist named Coeur de Roi managed to fall from the balcony at the first Orleans Theatre, friends held a concert to pay his medical bills. The audience was large, and also discreet enough to refrain from asking why the worthy Coeur de Roi had been hanging over the balcony in the first place.

Since music is the cause of the musicians' poverty, it stands to reason that benefit concerts are not the most effective means of assisting them in their plight. Recognizing this, members of the board of the New Orleans Symphony recently looked to nonmusical sources of support. They noticed that gambling is far more lucrative than classical music. So they organized the world's largest bingo game to benefit the heirs of Messrs. Passage and Coeur de Roi. Thinking big, they rented the entire Superdome, rolled up the astroturf, and set out a sea of tables across the football field. A clever idea, but would anyone come to the party?

Thousands of people were on hand even before the doors opened. They flooded in from suburbs with exotic names like Arabi, Fat City, Bucktown, and Westwego (named for a railroad line that headed west from the spot, hence "West we go"). Soon the entire floor area was packed, and bingo players began filling the stands. They played passionately, piercing the air with shrieks and groans as a funereal voice called out numbers over the public address system. Lulls in the bingo were devoted to bouts with cheap cardboard games that simulated the one-armed bandits of Las Vegas.

By the evening's end $89,000 was in the till. Another $1,700 in winnings had been turned back to the sponsors as contributions. This generous move, common at bingo evenings organized by local Catholic churches, reveals that the true gambler takes satisfaction from the game itself, and not from the crass hope of gain. As Shakespeare put it, "the play's the thing."

As the crowds filed out of the Dome, they left behind a floor ankle-deep in used bingo cards, discarded cardboard games, paper cups, hot dog wrappers, and spilled beer. The benefit had been a smashing success. One obviously contented patron was heard to ask her partner, "What's a symphony?" Monsieur Passage would have understood.

SINISTER POWERS

Something ominous looms in the very air of New Orleans, something sinister. In the clear and rational climate of Toronto, an unusual event can easily be dismissed as an accident or fluke. In the steamy and dank shadows of nocturnal New Orleans, the same event will be taken as evidence of Nature's irrational essence. Such a climate predisposes one to accept the possibility that macabre forces are at large in the world.

Back in 1918-19, an ax-wielding murderer terrorized the Carrollton district. This fellow had the nerve to write *The Times-Picayune* and report that the only people he would spare would be those in whose homes a jazz band was thundering away at the time of his arrival. Strangely, it never occurred to anyone to point the finger at the local musicians' union. Soon the threat subsided, however, although the case lives on in memory. Three generations later, there are still children shivering in their beds, in fear of the Axman.

The measure of New Orleanians' disbelief in a rational universe governed by Newtonian laws is their capacity for populating their environment with specters that spring from pure imagination. Such is the Lady in Violet of St. Roch Cemetery (pronounced St. Rock) in suburban Gentilly. Some years ago this neatly dressed matron hailed a cab at the cemetery gate and gave the driver an address. By the time the cab reached the house, the woman with the violet dress had disappeared. When the driver tried to collect his fare at the address he had been given, he was told that the woman in violet who fit his description had died several years earlier. But she's still active in the locale, much to the chagrin of Neighborhood Watch.

More eerie yet is the Gown Man, or "Gowman," as his name is pronounced. Older residents have assured this writer that the Gowman dresses in white and hides at night in the leafy trees along Esplanade Avenue in order to leap down on his victims, murder them, and steal their corpses.

Who is the Gowman? He sounds suspiciously like a medical student. Everyone knows, of course, that medical students cut up cadavers. What is less clear, at least to those who conceived of Gowman, is where they get the corpses in the first place. Spokespersons for local hospitals explained the complex process by which they acquire cadavers, the legal protections that they obtain, and so forth. Obviously, this struck a certain part of the population as pure poppycock. They knew that there was a Gowman out there somewhere, and the fact that they had not actually seen him merely proved that he was stealthy and clever.

Among those who respect the Gowman's powers is a well-known jazz trumpeter, who shall go unnamed. Although a good Catholic, he always asks his friends to drive him straight to his door at night, lest the Gowman pounce down upon him. The tactic has been eminently successful, for our musician is now in his seventies and is still going strong. But so is the macabre specter in the trees outside the musician's home.

TACKLING FATE

The realization that life is unpredictable can lead one in many directions. Some choose to live only for the present, reveling in sybaritic pleasures. Others wallow in the uncertainty of it all by indulging in games of chance. A few hearty souls try to gain the upper hand.

The indirect method of doing this is to become a scientist, to study geology, metereology, or epidemiology, and to use that knowledge to anticipate the next disaster before it happens. The direct method is far simpler: to propitiate the forces of evil and get them on your side.

This was Faust's approach, and it worked fairly well for a while. But Faust's Satan spoke German and would therefore be unable to understand messages from Orleans Parish. The best way to hook up with the powers of darkness in New Orleans has been through voodoo.

This subject has long since been usurped by the guidebook writers. After all, the writhing snakes, cauldrons of frogs, unguents and *gris-gris* make good copy. Since the topic is dead, let us state simply that those wishing to pay their respects to the city's voodoo queens may visit the tomb of the famous Marie Laveau (there were three queens by this name) in St. Louis Cemetery No. 2—if they can find it. Or they may visit the Glapion family tomb in St. Louis Cemetery No. 1, which may contain the remains of Marie Laveau's mother, Marie I. Knock three times.

Organized voodoo is a thing of the past, but more than a few do-it-yourself practitioners live on. It may be pranksters who are marking crosses in brick dust on the Laveau tomb these days, but it was certainly not practical jokers who deposited broken china and packs of pins and needles on several graves in Carrollton Cemetery No. 1 recently. And who is it who left potatoes that had been scooped out and filled with salt on several tombs in St. Louis No. 2, and even small handmade dolls?

A mathematician from New Orleans recalls taking his general examinations for the Ph.D. at Tulane back in the early '60s. His grandmother, herself a well-educated woman, took the precaution of lighting several voodoo candles on the eve of the fateful day. In the same vein, Nils Bohr, the physicist and Nobel laureate from Denmark, is reported to have hung a horseshoe above his door.

"Do you believe in that?" someone asked Bohr.

"No," he replied, "but you never can tell."

Advertisement: Mother Margaret, spiritual reader and healer, guarantees "to remove evil influences and bad luck." She can be reached at 3300 South Broad Street, New Orleans, 70125.

SAINT EXPEDITE

Every old Catholic community worth its salt has at least one local saint. New Orleans has several, although none has yet been recognized by Rome, or by the local Archdiocese, for that matter.

If any of them deserves full canonization and veneration in the modern world, it is surely St. Expedite. The shrine to this little-known patron of the U.S. Post Office is situated in the Church of Our Lady of Guadalupe on North Rampart Street. Forsooth, St. Expedite was created on that very spot.

It seems that a large icon that had been ordered for the sanctuary was delivered in a strong wooden packing crate. Aside from the address of the church the only marking on the crate was the word EXPEDITE in large stenciled letters. Hence, the name.

One can easily imagine what might have happened had the carton been labeled FRAGILE.

VII

SURREALISM

In which a pompous French conceit
is invoked to explain
the unreality of reality
in the Crescent City.

Her Majesty's raiment

SURREALISM

Scholars claim that Surrealism was invented by the French poet André Breton in 1924. Surrealists shocked good burghers by announcing that the real is unreal, that the world as we see it is nonsense, and that only what we feel intuitively really exists.

Now, Breton was clever but he should not be given all the posies, for New Orleans has been turning its whole population into surrealists for a century. They do not think of themselves as surrealists, and some may invite you to step outside if you call them that. Nonetheless, you may be sure they are convinced believers in the doctrine.

Here's how Jelly Roll Morton tried to explain the fact that the so-called "second line" of dancers in funeral parades actually marched out front: "It's a funny thing that the second line marched at the head of the parade, *but that's the way it had to be in New Orleans.*" A ludicrous explanation, to be sure. But, then what is one to make of a city in which South Rampart Street is upriver of North Rampart Street; in which there never was a coliseum on Coliseum Street nor a canal on Canal Street or even on Canal Avenue; in which Prytania Street memorializes a nonexistent Prytanèe, or school; in which one reaches the *west* bank of the river by going due east across the Mississippi River Bridge; and in which the sun rises over the west bank? There should have been no surprise when Charles Dudley Warner, visiting the Deep South in 1887, wrote "I never could find out exactly where New Orleans is."

The unreality of reality in New Orleans extends to the very plan of the city. Superficially it appears to have been built on a rational Cartesian grid. But because of the bend in the river, the entire grid is skewed. Hence, in a bizarre tribute to non-Euclidean geometry, parallel lines can meet in New Orleans. Which accounts for the fact that it is easy to become completely disoriented in the Crescent City, both literally and figuratively.

Look with your own eyes. Is it not true that Canal Street and St. Charles Street meet at right angles? It is equally self-evident that both thoroughfares head out from their point of junction in straight lines. Then how is it that Carrollton Avenue (which clearly joins St. Charles Avenue at a ninety-degree turn and runs straight thereafter) connects eventually with Canal Street, and at another right angle? Stated formally, $90°+90°=270°$, in New Orleans, at least. Two times two might as well equal five.

There are still stranger things to behold. Ships churning along the Mississippi look *down* on New Orleans rooftops; large houses have no other contact with *terra firma* than a few fragile piers of brick, which leave clear sky visible beneath the structures; and during the early spring nearly the entire city is known to disappear completely in a swirl of fog. Then there is the preposterous pseudo-French Quarter building that can be seen from Camp Street perched precariously atop the Monteleone Hotel, and the Roman temple surmounting the Hibernia Bank Building.

New Orleanians, it seems, perceive naturally what French intellects toiled to explain by writing books that are largely forgotten today. Mr. Breton could have saved himself a lot of trouble by visiting the Crescent City, and he would have had a good time besides.

BALLET DE COUR

Reality and unreality meet in strange ways. A while back a New Orleans woman received a traffic ticket for speeding through the blocks of bars and used auto parts stores in suburban Kenner. Since fixing tickets is as American as apple pie, she naturally contacted a friend who had a friend, etc. It was easily seen to. The only price she had to pay was to arrange for a "call out." This, in effect, was her bill.

To understand the lady's tariff, we must digress. In the time of Louis XIV, ballet was all the rage at the French court. With nothing better to do after dinner, the lords and ladies of the realm would choose an exotic theme, dress themselves up in costumes and masks, and act it out. After the initial grand march, it was all rather stilted. The idea was to form moving pictures or scenes from mythology and history. Such dramatizations were called *tableaux,* and they did much to develop the art of ballet.

Everyone got into the act back then. Louis himself became known as "The Sun King" because he acted (or danced) the role of the sun in one such *ballet de cour.* The high point of the evening would occur when the king's chamberlain "called out" prominent lady aristocrats from the audience and asked them to join the masked actors-dancers-aristocrats on the floor. Only Important People received this honor, and they vied for it.

Now back to Louisiana. The French *ballet de cour* arrived in Creole New Orleans in the eighteenth century, complete with grand march and "call outs." The Anglo-Saxons adapted it to their own Mardi Gras balls a century later. Then it spread out into the suburbs, eventually reaching Kenner, near the airport.

The price for fixing that speeding ticket was to arrange things so that the middleman's wife would receive a "call-out" at a Mardi Gras ball. Not one of the fancy "up-town" balls, either, but a down-home suburban one of the sort where the men wear frilly baby-blue shirts with their tuxedos and the women look like Dolly Parton. Recognition by the masked oligarchs of Kenner should not be sneezed at, however, for a "call out" is like old gold, maintaining its value over the years, through bull and bear markets. An investment in "call out" futures would be a good hedge against inflation.

Mardi Gras is many things. In its public manifestations, it is a boon to the tourist industry. Its numerous private balls are a light-hearted game for the participants. For many members of New Orleans' large and sophisticated Jewish community, Mardi Gras is something to be ignored, preferably by leaving town. More than one critic has argued that Mardi Gras diverts private resources from other worthwhile forms of community activity.

All this may be true. But Mardi Gras is also a city-wide indulgence in pure fantasy that has no parallel on the entire North American continent. At Mardi Gras balls the accountant emerges as a prancing satyr and your friendly tax lawyer steps out as an elegant mime from the *Ancien Régime*.

Not that most of the participants know or care what happened at the court of Louis XIV, or by what process that custom from the remote past was transmitted to New Orleans and eventually to Kenner. They don't. And their indifference on this point is sure proof that the annual rite is real, not an antiquarian affectation. Through Mardi Gras, the wife of the ticket-fixer in Kenner, Louisiana briefly ascends, via Airline Highway, to an ethereal realm of baroque fantasy.

MASQUE

Jack Henry Abbott, former convict, author of *In the Belly of the Beast* and Norman Mailer's literary protégé, was on the run. Released from prison for good behavior, he stabbed a man in a New York coffee shop dispute over access to a rest room. The man died. So Abbott headed for New Orleans as fast as he could.

Only at this point did his actions become noteworthy. Abbot needed a cover. Having just read John Kennedy Toole's *Confederacy of Dunces*, he decided to follow its hero and sign up to sell foot-long hot dogs out of a weenie-shaped pushcart. This was admittedly no stroke of genius but it did reveal a degree of understanding. For in a city of maskers, only the unmasked stands out.

No American city is more hospitable to those reptilian souls who wish to shed their old skin and try a new one. New Orleans is an international capital of transformations, presided over by the god of change, Proteus, who is honored each year with a parade at Carnival time.

Mardi Gras is itself a festival of transformation, a time when adults become children and children become adults. In olden days the masks revealed more about the maskers than did their everyday identities. Prostitutes dressed as sailors and sailors as captains or pirates. Poor blacks masked as stock brokers or kings, and mortgage bankers became cutthroats or bums.

People usually trade up when they mask. That's why there are so many kings, dukes, and tinsel royalty at Carnival. For at bottom, few of America's professed Jeffersonians are all that firm in their democratic faith. One recalls that when architectural plans were solicited for the White House during the administration of George Washington, one of the entries called for a throne room.

Masking is not confined to the pre-Lenten season. Confucian sages, Elizabethan duchesses and hundreds of blacks masked as Indians—the "Yellow Tchoupitoulas," "Golden Stars," and other "tribes"—pop up at festivities throughout the year. Nor is masking even limited to the society of mortal humans. In New Orleans, even houses mask. The humble shotgun dwelling is so named because you could fire a gun from the front door out the back, through all the lined-up rooms. Built of wood, the shotgun house was the stationary antecedent of the lowly house trailer of today. But with a few columns and a cartload of turned finials and jigsaw lacework, Victorian builders could enable the shotgun house to step out as a Venetian palace or a Grecian temple.

To be sure, anyone who steps around to the back of the shotgun house can readily see that no Grand Doge or Pericles would ever have set foot in such a place. The humdrum cypress siding reminds us that the transformation is less than complete. But do you really want to see that shotgun house with its facade off? Or the masked concubine clad in her housedress doing the dishes in Metairie? Or Jack Abbott as he really was, morosely sipping coffee at the Hummingbird Grill on St. Charles Street as the FBI closed in on him?

If you do, if you actually prefer to see the world this way, then you should at least permit your victims to unmask you in return.

BALANCE OF PAYMENTS

"The queen's collar was composed of fifteen wine-red French plumes. Her mantle was velvet, heavily encrusted with beads and rhinestones and trimmed in ermine. [She wore a] bouffant satin gown with an overskirt of *point d'esprit* featuring a panel of rhinestones on the asymmetrical tier of chiffon. The sweetheart bodice of brocade was heavily encrusted with silver fringe pearls, aurora borealis stones, sequins, and bugle beads."

> ~ Description of costume worn by the queen of the Krewe of Nefertiti, a carnival organization for black women.
>
> (*Times-Picayune*, February 20, 1982.)

INFRASTRUCTURE

Any human institution can be viewed from the outside or the inside, from above or below. It's one thing, for example, to sigh through Swan Lake and quite another to watch those sylph-like dancers toss down a TV dinner between performances. Mr. Tchaikovsky might deny it, but both vistas are equally real.

New Orleans, a city that lives on and for the outside, has as complex an inner structure as does the Statue of Liberty. Under the surface sheen are tens and even hundreds of work-a-day souls whose toil makes the whole thing happen. Enter the kitchen of any restaurant and you'll see them, members of a veritable army of cooks and waiters. Serving them in turn is a batallion of provisioners, working from the uncharted wilds of New Orleans East. These in turn are sustained by further regiments of truck farmers and fishermen working from bases across South Louisiana. They truly constitute an "army." When the Civil War broke out, the Croatian shrimpers of Plaquemines Parish organized themselves into a shrimpers' regiment within the Confederate forces.

Simply to chart the organization of such infrastructures would tax the ingenuity of the Harvard Business School. Musicians are banded together in Local 174-496 of the American Federation of Musicians. If you need forty-nine tuba players or eighteen tambourine players, the Local can provide them. Like the waiters, the musicians have their own complex pecking order, which is replicated in miniature among those who play each instrument. And everybody knows who's who.

To mask the thousands of members of the various Carnival krewes and other Mardi Gras revelers, hundreds of seamstresses keep busy year round. For more ordinary revelers there is the MGM Costume Shop, Regal Clothes, and the grand old Carnival outfitter, Irving Gerson at Jo-Ann Costumes on Dryades Street. At peak season Mr. Gerson employs a staff of fifteen. On short notice he can provide a King Arthur costume or a grass skirt for a member of the Zulu Social Aid and Pleasure Club.

A short list of industries that thrive in New Orleans but that have few parallels elsewhere are carriage repair shops (for the mule-drawn surreys that ply the Vieux Carre; importers and manufacturers of Mardi Gras beads and doubloons; float designers; sequin and feather boa wholesalers; T-shirt and poster manufacturers; bakers who specialize in King Cakes (the German *Kaiserkuchen*) and fancy breads for St. Joseph's Day; embroiderers of banners; praline cooks; calligraphers versed in the art of drafting proclamations; and choreographers for the baroque masques. All this exists in the twentieth century.

Lurking out of sight behind the visible part of the frivolity industry stands an invisible group of specialists who discreetly provide every manner of service. How should an *ersatz* duchess comport herself? There are those who will coach her. And what do you do with a $4,000 gown after the big night? Over on Claiborne Avenue is a woman who will arrange for it to be recycled for the benefit of some future reveler in the New Orleans suburb of Arabi or even Mobile.

When the *Ancien Régime* in France toppled in 1789, the infrastructure of baroque life died with it. When the Romanoffs lost their throne in Russia, the Fabergés did not last a week. It was all very sad. But New Orleans shows that history can repeat itself—if not as tragedy, then as farce.

ALLEGORY

"Mardi Gras," fumed the *Delta* in 1853, "has become vulgar, tasteless...." Does this sound familiar? Defenders of Carnival avoid facing such criticism frontally. Instead, they raise a fog of irrelevant issues. Mardi Gras is fun, they assert, which is undeniable if you enjoy such things. It's good for business, too, they claim. Not that the Avondale Shipyards receives huge orders from drunken revelers, mind you. But the carousers have to sleep somewhere, and find something to wash down with all the potables.

Others respond to the criticism of Mardi Gras by defending it as a kind of public therapy that helps local folk muddle through even the worst of times with silly grins on their faces. There's something to this, as any New Orleanian who lived through the Depression here can verify. But the argument sometimes ends up on its head. The famous Mardi Gras of 1838, for example, saw one of the first true parades. But it did not follow the collapse of fourteen local banks, as some authorities have claimed, but preceded it, and not by long, either. It leaves one very suspicious.

But let us admit that Mardi Gras is the best thing for the psyche since the long defunct but now partially resurrected local soft drink, Dr. Nut. Is it not vulgar and tasteless nonetheless? Some learned professors of revelry answer yes, yes, a thousand times yes. They wallow in the sleaziness of the streets, the tawdry masques, the drunkenness. All vulgarity is not equal, they say. Mardi Gras is the genuine article, true-life vulgarity rather than the fake and sanitized version dished up to American homes by television. It's real, and therefore good.

Hogwash with a Ph.D. is still hogwash, and the *Delta*'s charge remains unanswered. Is Mardi Gras vulgar and tasteless? A serious response emerges from the list of decidedly un-vulgar themes of the parades over the years—the parades being the heart of the modern Carnival. Typical samples are "Tales of Gilgamesh," "The World's Worships," and "Tales of Josephus." One must be a certified classicist just to figure the box score.

But surely all this has changed in modern times? In Part, yes. The genuine vulgarity of Hollywood sets the taste of the suburban parades and for at least one of the major downtown parades these days. But the solid old Krewe of Comus, founded in 1857 and named after an early work of John Milton, sticks to traditional themes. Take just the year 1982, when its theme was "Ophidian Lore." To save a trip to the *Encyclopedia Britannica*, this refers to the suborder *ophidia*, which comprises all snakes. Hence Comus produced floats on "Eden," "Aesculapius," "Dumbala," "Abraxas," and "Python." The latter, by the way, is not your garden variety *ophidium* but the mythical dragon that guarded ancient Delphi, the source of prophetic vapors.

Now imagine hundreds of thousands of potbellied rednecks from Mississippi, North Florida and Manhattan lining up to watch some New Orleans businessmen represent all this allegorically. Picture businessmen anywhere dressing in outlandish costumes in order to present samples of Ophidian Lore to the masses, and paying every penny of the costs to do so. It staggers the imagination.

Which is precisely what Mardi Gras is all about. Beneath the superficial vulgarity, it is a poetic festival steeped in the exquisite high art of allegory. The right theme can produce floats of dizzying abstraction, such as "The Whirlwind of Fire" based on a story by an ancient Roman writer. Unfortunately, a reckless *flambeaux* carrier almost turned that particular *papier-mâché* fantasy into the real thing.

Nor is Mardi Gras without uplifting moral content. For instance, the black Zulu Social Aid and Pleasure Club in 1938 took for its theme "The Prince and the Demon." Every conceivable temptation was presented allegorically, but in the end the prince triumphed over Evil. Any spectator who thoughtfully pondered the deeper message of Zulu in 1938 would have immediately become a better person. Provided, of course, that he was sober.

FILIBUSTERS

Human beings come in two types. There are the down-to-earth practical folks who deal with the world as they find it. Then there are dreamers, for whom nothing is more real than the technicolor chimeras that flash before their imaginations. Both sorts exist in the Crescent City, but New Orleans is the national capital only for the second type.

For the true visionary, all the world's a stage and he is the playwright. His ultimate triumph is to remake everyday reality to fit his fancy. This eventually leads him to politics, not of your everyday garden variety, but revolutionary utopias. And what better place to conjure up a revolution than over a glass or two at a good New Orleans bar?

This is precisely what "General" Narciso Lopez, a Venezuelan, did in the 1850's. Making his headquarters at Banks' Arcade off Poydras Street, Lopez attempted the conquest of Cuba from New Orleans. He failed, but that only whetted the city's appetite for vicarious adventure.

Lopez' choice of Banks' Arcade was not fortuitous. Mr. Thomas Banks himself, an entrepreneur, had mounted his own political opera when he and some cronies plotted the Texas revolution from a tavern on the premises.

A doctor's office at the foot of Canal Street provided the setting for one of the most bizarre political operettas ever staged in New Orleans. William Walker, bored by his practice of both medicine and law, proposed to seize Nicaragua and settle it with his own chorus of extras. He failed of course, for the script demands that all such buffo adventures fall to earth in the end.

Walker and Lopez were "filibusters," a charming old word that once referred to political buccaneers of the Caribbean. Now such people have settled in Washington.

But not all of them. In 1983 three score fighters set sail from New Orleans to do battle with the Sandinista government in Nicaragua. This turned out to be a fairly humdrum mission and its collapse was predictable. A less routine project was mounted in 1980, when an unlikely band of Ku Klux Klansmen, drug dealers, black terrorists, and gamblers plotted to seize the 300-square mile island of Dominica, which lies between Guadeloupe and Martinique. The idea was simple: take over the island and set it up as a tropical paradise for drugs and gambling. But the libretto was tawdry, a comic-book parody of New Orleans' splendidly absurd political operettas of old. Needless to say, this attempted coup was a failure.

The so-called "Bayou of Pigs" scheme had only one small redeeming touch: the 52-foot charter boat on which the filibusters were to set sail from New Orleans was appropriately named the "Mañana."

FIXED COSTS

In which, by an original calculus,
less is shown to produce more
in New Orleans and adjacent parishes,
and with predictable consequences
for all.

Un-haughty cuisine

FIXED COSTS

A laconic young New Englander in his twenties was recently seen in a small park along Elysian Fields, pondering a paperback copy of *How to Get Rich and Remain Happy*. Under questioning, he revealed that he was a salesman paid on commission. His boss wanted him to work harder, and promised up to twice his present income if he did so. But the young man confessed that he already had all that he required to live comfortably in New Orleans. His boss, a penetrating student of political economy, stated the matter succinctly:

"Your fixed costs are too low."

What the boss presumably meant was that if the man would only increase his monthly expenses, he would then need more income and hence would work harder to obtain it. One can imagine Henry David Thoreau getting the same advice from a shopkeeper in Concord. And indeed there are striking parallels between Thoreau's stripped-down existence at Walden Pond and the lives of tens of thousands of New Orleanians.

Thoreau, for example, took pride in his simplified diet, which consisted of beans, peas, rice, pork, and watermelon. Assuming that his pork was in sausage form, Thoreau merely "discovered" the staple New Orleans dish of beans and rice. Since the hardships of the Civil War had not yet forced the McIlhenny family into manufacturing their world-renowned Tabasco Sauce, Thoreau cannot be blamed for leaving it off his menu.

To house himself at Walden Pond, Thoreau looked for the cheapest used materials. For $425 he purchased a certain James Collins' shanty along the Fitchburg Railroad and dismantled it for its boards and nails. These Thoreau rebuilt into his own dwelling. Meanwhile, long before Thoreau's architectural efforts, New Orleanians had been buying used flatboats from the rivermen and tearing them apart for lumber. Many of these cheap "barge board houses" can still be seen in the city's Irish Channel section. Except that they are slightly larger than the shack at Walden, these and thousands of other New Orleans shotgun houses are strikingly similar in their overall form to Thoreau's own cottage and are at least as effective a way to reduce fixed costs.

Other happy factors conspire to reduce the fixed costs of low-income New Orleanians. Louisiana license plates proclaim the state to be a "Sportsman's Paradise." What this means is that one can easily supplement one's diet by hunting and fishing. And, too, the fairly even climate spares one the need to maintain three costly changes of clothes for the passing seasons.

All of this contributes to a sense of ease, born of the confidence that anyone wishing to do so can get by on little money. As the poet Goethe said of Naples, "here it is enough for contentment if a man has ever so little income."

New Orleans is not lacking in poverty. But nature and culture join forces to relieve the poor and subsidize the Bohemian. And those low fixed costs mean an equally low level of striving. As America's great landscape architect, Frederick Law Olmsted observed of New Orleans in 1867, "Everybody lives freer and spends their money more willingly here." And so they do, as much today as in the past. It is "The Big Easy."

INGESTION

General Benjamin F. Butler, commandant of the federal occupational forces in New Orleans during the Civil War, was as unlovable a fellow as one could hope to find. His family profiteered shamelessly. He treated illustrious citizens with what they considered to be draconian severity. He even insulted the ladies of New Orleans. He had pendent jowls and they called him "The Beast." He had another nickname as well: "Spoons." This epithet arose when it was rumored around town that he had made off with silverware from the luxurious home on Camp Street which he had commandeered for himself. Few have heard of "The Beast" today. But everyone knows of the nefarious "Spoons."

It is revealing that Butler could hang a New Orleanian in the courtyard of the old Mint on Esplanade Avenue and almost get away with it. But let anyone suggest that he committed the slightest crime at the dinner table and his memory is reviled through the ages. For in New Orleans, eating is almost as important as life itself. More important, perhaps.

The oyster, for example, is well known as an unparalleled source of cholesterol. Fry the oyster and you have a lethal weapon, a kind of crustacian neutron bomb aimed at the circulatory system. If food were not more important than life, would New Orleanians dare eat oysters in such prodigious quantities?

Eating in New Orleans is not something you do in order to be able to pursue other activities, but the reverse. Neither religion, sex, nor even politics can compete with food as a topic of conversation. And not just before dinner as the juices flow, either. Pull back the chairs after a four-course groaner at K-Paul's or Dooky Chase's and what will the company discuss? Food.

Small wonder, then, that New Orleanians consume more bread, coffee, and alcohol per capita than residents of any other American city. To find another population so addicted to ingestion one has to turn back to Victorian times—perhaps to Dickens' Pickwick Club, which, incidentally, gave its name to one of the first men's clubs founded in New Orleans. And that was no accident.

Statistics compiled by *New Orleans* magazine provide solid support for New Orleans' claims to being the North American capital of *gourmandisme*. The average Crescent City resident eats 15 lunches and 10.9 dinners out each month. These aren't snacks, either. The average breakfast bill is $5.17 and for lunch it is $7.44. Thirty percent of the respondents organize catered meals at least once a year and fully forty-three percent annually reserve a private room in a restaurant.

As to the cuisine, fried seafood far outranks everything else, including fast food and Chinese delicacies. Health food is at the very bottom of the list, with a paltry four-tenths of a percent of New Orleanians' restaurant meals. No wonder the British novelist William Makepeace Thackeray called New Orleans "the city of the world where you can eat and drink the most and suffer the least." This, at least, is what seems to happen.

The only topic that can come close to rivaling food as a subject of conversation is dieting. There is no pill or powder for the reduction of blubber that has not been tested by tens of thousands of New Orleanians. But the addiction to eating is not so easily thwarted. And not just among the affluent. Eddie's, a modest-looking but distinguished black Creole restaurant in the city's Seventh Ward, serves portions that demand long periods of the strictest training to handle. And Rocky and Carlo's, a restaurant-bar across from the sprawling Kaiser Aluminum plant in Chalmette, has created a new race of working men and women who are easily recognized by their absence of necks and waistlines and by their multiple chins. More's the pity that Mario Gioe, a part owner of Rocky and Carlo's, was recently put away in an execution-style gangland slaying out on East Judge Perez Drive.

This is not the place to consider the fine points of New Orleans cuisine. The last word on that subject was said in 1903 anyway, by the *Times-Picayune* in its now reprinted classic cookbook. Let it be noted simply that the city has no indigenous *haute cuisine*. The finest Creole dishes were—and are—served up in private homes by black Creole chefs, who prepare the same fare for their own families. *Grillades* in the Garden District taste the same as *grillades* in Faubourg Marigny. And so does the diet drink the next day.

FREE LUNCH (AND DINNER)

It should surprise no one that there *is* a free lunch in New Orleans. Less well known is the fact that it was invented there. And then it was partially reinvented a century later, creating a legacy that survives to our day.

The old St. Louis Hotel stood where the Royal Orleans Hotel is today, smack in the heart of the French Quarter. One of its arcaded walls was incorporated into the modern building. Under the grand cupola of the St. Louis, slaves were sold at auction in the nineteenth century. Philippe Alvarez ran the hotel's bar nearby. Whether because of the loathsome trade going on under the cupola or because of the continuing effects of the nationwide financial panic of 1837, guests just weren't drinking. Alvarez therefore decided to lure them with free snacks, in the hope that these would generate a camel's thirst. Alvarez rightly calculated that guests would open their wallets to satisfy their thirst. Thus, the free snacks soon became whole lunches—very salty ones, presumably.

Nearly a century later, in 1930, the brothers Benny and Clovis Martin kept a neighborhood restaurant out on St. Claude Avenue. Benny and Clovis had once worked as streetcar motormen. When Streetcar Union No. 194 went out on strike, the Martins, sympathizing with their former co-workers, resolved to feed "the poor boys" free. Local 194 eventually went back to work, but the overstuffed sandwiches the Martins served its members live on.

According to the definitive history of the subject by New Orleans journalist Bunny Matthews, some seventeen million loaves of "Po-Boy" bread are still produced each year by the Reising Bakery. Donald de Fresne, proprietor of the Friendly House Restaurant, serves up several thousands of these, and de Fresne is but one of hundreds of purveyors to their majesties, the citizens of New Orleans. Few of the Po-Boys concocted by the Martins or de Fresne are given away free these days, but they are still one of the genuine gastronomic bargains of the United States.

HEART-WARMER

Homo *Novo-Orleanensis* likes to drink. He drinks in the morning, afternoon, and evening. He drinks the national standards, and also more rarefied local fare: Ramos fizzes, Sazerac cocktails, and green opal suissesses. He drinks standing, sitting, and driving. In 1981 a bill was introduced in the Louisiana Senate banning open beverage containers from the streets. New Orleans' Senator Nat Kiefer averred that "this goes much too far."

Strangely, most of the world's serious drinkers are Northerners. Finns, Swedes, Russians, and Vermonters use liquor to fortify themselves against the cold. That alcohol can also be used for exactly the opposite purpose warrants further study, possibly at the Good Timers Bar on St. Bernard Avenue, at Uncle Henry's on Banks Street, at Munster's on Lyons Street, or at Myrt and Vic's in Algiers. Such experiments are in fact underway.

Drinking constitutes one of those rare islands of permanence in the evanescent life of New Orleans. But, alas, the pall of mortality casts its shadow even over the bent elbow. Gone is Jax Beer, not to mention the once-plentiful berry wines and other locally produced goods. One local drink—the immensely popular absinthe— had the honor of having been banned by an act of the U.S. Senate.

Absinthe, or something like it, is mentioned in the Bible (Matt. XXIII, 23). The major ingredients of this yellowish-green drink are anise and wormwood, the latter also mentioned in the Bible (Rev. VIII, 11). Wormwood, a bitter additive, is squeezed from roots of a squattish shrub, *artemisia absinthium*. It sharpens the flavor of true absinthe. It is also habit-forming, giving rise to delirium and hallucinations, and eventually causing permanent mental deterioration. From 1837, when the first absinthe was brewed in New Orleans, to February 12, 1912, when it was banned, each bottle contained several drops of wormwood.

The ban irked New Orleanians. Since almost all American absinthe was both produced and consumed in the Crescent City, the government's intervention seemed punitive. Mental deterioration is inevitable anyway, New Orleanians argued, so why shouldn't one be free to choose a pleasant route to oblivion? Besides, they noted, since absinthe is 100 to 180 proof, the alcohol would have done its work long before the effects of the wormwood could be discerned.

Meanwhile, members of the New Orleans Absinthe Manufacturers Association figured out a means of producing absinthe without wormwood. For twenty-two years after the ban they produced this substitute in epic quantities, to the delight of local imbibers. But according to the federal legislation, absinthe without wormwood wasn't absinthe. So the local industry took its case to the Louisiana State Board of

Health. On the morning of July 10, 1934, the State Chemist presided over an official tasting. A bottle of true absinthe was produced, and a bottle of Herbsaint, the stuff without wormwood. Ice, seltzer, and simple syrup were there—everything needed to make an absinthe frappe.

The glasses were filled with cracked ice, then a teaspoon of syrup. Into the first glass went a jigger of absinthe, while a jigger of Herbsaint went into the second. Seltzer followed in both, producing the familiar cloudy marine color. Then the chemist, lawyers, stenographers, and reporters dipped in. To their amazement, they could not distinguish between the two drinks.

History does not record how that morning ended in 1934. With the absinthe at over 100 proof, one can imagine. It must have been like Stockholm, Helsinki, or Moscow at the winter solstice. But in the end, federal law prevailed. Hence absinthe is absent from New Orleans, although Herbsaint is still there, as are bourbon, scotch, gin, vodka, wine, etc.

WORKING

Of all Southern cities, New Orleans is unique in having had a large working class from its earliest days. Its immigrant workers and freedmen made it a working man's town when most Southern "cities" were little more than administrative or market centers.

Given this, it is all the more surprising that the much-vaunted American work ethic has made so few inroads along the Mississippi's *batture*. But such is the case. *Poor Richard* would roll over in his grave at the sight of New Orleanians arriving late to the job, leaving early, and enjoying three-Sazerac lunches in between. Nor can such practices be blamed on the muggy climate. True, the mere contemplation of nature's open-air steam bath beyond the plate glass window is debilitating, while the prospect of traversing the sweltering gauntlet between air-conditioned home and air-conditioned office can turn grown men into foot-dragging school boys.

But the same leisurely work habits persist in the winter months as well. In some quarters, it's best not even to attempt to transact major business between Twelfth Night and Ash Wednesday, while Carnival bubbles away. This alone knocks almost three months out of the work year. Then subtract the period of preparation for Carnival, which extends from Thanksgiving through Christmas, and the work year ends up a scrawny skeleton.

This is not to imply that New Orleanians set speed records on the job the rest of the time. An official at the Labor Department in the state capital at Baton Rouge confirms that factory discipline in New Orleans is weak, and that the productivity of labor there is so low that more than one potential investor has been scared away from the city.

Should responsibility for this be laid on the educational system? Maybe. When they built the Marriott Hotel on Canal Street, some of the local laborers had to be sent home and replaced with better-trained and more highly-motivated workers from the outside. But many of the same work habits are evident in the front office as well, where the staffs are presumably better educated.

Leisurely work habits are even to be found in the august world of banking. What young banker has not been told that the "three C's" of his profession are cash, credit and collateral? In New Orleans banks the three C's were long said to be "clubs, contacts and Carnival," scarcely an adage worth quoting, perhaps, were it not for the fact that some New Orleans bankers themselves do so. Such attitudes can even influence the credit operations of banks. During the recent recession an enterprising gentleman dropped by the city's most venerable bank for a business loan. They dismissed his request out of hand, saying that the times just weren't ripe for new projects. "But if you're interested in a loan to cover your daughter's coming out, let us know...." Play is a safer risk than work.

Much work does get done in New Orleans. The evidence is on every side. Multinational corporations have been built here, and vigorous local industries turn out products that are sold around the world. But for all this, the city provides a useful footnote to the famous thesis of German sociologist Max Weber (1864-1920) regarding the so-called "Protestant ethic." According to Weber, capitalism boomed wherever the Protestant emphasis upon work held sway. But Weber failed to notice the obvious fact that all of those hardworking Protestants were also northerners, whether in Europe or America. Nature made their fixed costs high; to survive, they *had* to work.

One wonders what would have happened if those northerners infected with Weber's work ethic had been transplanted wholesale into Naples, Barcelona, or New Orleans. How long would their passion for productivity have survived ?

DRIVERS

There are many reasons for not leaving New Orleans once you are there. One of the most compelling is that, as a driver, it may cost you your life. The New Orleans driver on his home turf is dangerous enough. If he practices his usual habits anywhere else, however, he will become a Haspel-suited Kamikaze pilot.

To set the civic chauvanists at rest, New Orleanians are not the most aggressive drivers. Bostonians claim that honor. Nor are they the most surly (Philadelphia's prize); the most selfish (Washington, D.C.); the fastest (Los Angeles); or the most given to using their horns (New York). But New Orleanians are not without honor, for they are undoubtedly the most whimsical drivers in the land.

Where else do people make a habit of parking on the left side of two-lane streets? Where will you see so many fanciful turns from wrong lanes? Such daring broken-field maneuvers? Where do drivers take such keen interest in the passing flora and fauna? Amazingly, all this is accomplished at the wheels of lumbering gas-guzzlers, still by far the preferred mode of transportation throughout the Oil Belt.

In an age of conformity, New Orleans drivers are individualists. They set their speed according to their personal metabolisms, racing and slowing down with the tempo of their inner thoughts. They are the last devotees of hand signals, each driver devising his own private code of gestures. Between mimetic exhibitions, the left arm is used to beat out the tempo set by gospel disc jockeys on WVOG or WSHO or by country music from WNOE.

Such creative inner directedness is no mean feat, considering that each driver is simultaneously dodging potholes, streetcars, and equally whimsical pedestrians. All of this takes years of practice and should not be attempted by new arrivals, however envious they may be.

Isn't such creative use of the automobile dangerous, you ask? Definitely. Is it accidental that driver's licenses and hunting licenses are both available in Louisiana at bargain-basement prices? They are easily confused. Unfortunately, though, "traffic statisticians" at the Police Department can provide no quantitative measure of how dangerous it is to drive in New Orleans other than to show with figures that it is perilous to be either a driver or a pedestrian here.

One surprise the statistics do reveal, however, is that rush hours are a relatively safe time to drive in New Orleans and that weekdays are safer than Saturdays. The most dangerous times to be on the road are the periods between two and four p.m. and two and four a.m. These are the hours when New Orleanians are most reflective. As they muse over the redfish off Grand Isle, or Aunt Dolores' last trip to Opelousas, or L.S.U.'s new backfield coach, they sink into a private world in which stop signs, traffic lanes and policemen's frowns have no place. That's the time to watch out.

In their behalf, it must be acknowledged that New Orleans drivers do not consider the automobile to be an instrument of creative expression. They drive to the music of their own whimsy.

MENTAL HEALTH

Is New Orleans really the "City That Care Forgot"? Is it truly "The Big Easy," as the travel posters proclaim? Or could these labels be applied just as accurately to Newark, San Jose, or Toledo?

Lawsuits over false advertising can be messy, so it is high time these questions are answered, soberly and scientifically. Health statistics are called for—computerized print-outs covering every man, woman and child from Chalmette to River Ridge. Reams of them. Such data should be readily at hand, since Louisiana has virtually free medical care for anyone needing it, a legacy of Huey Long.

"What, if anything, is really different about New Orleanians, physiologically and mentally?" Presented with this query, a respected epidemiologist instantly shot back, "Diabetes and pancreatic cancer." And so they are. But upon closer inspection, these diseases turn out to be problems throughout south Louisiana, not just in The Big Easy. So we are no closer to an answer.

A psychiatrist who has worked with the statistics for twenty years had an even more depressing response. "Hysteria," he coolly replied, "just like in rural Mexico or Guatemala." More good news for the Chamber of Commerce.

Perhaps such data are too general, too lacking in real-life detail. Fortunately, the State of Louisiana maintains a series of neighborhood mental health clinics throughout the Crescent City. Hundreds of clergymen are also in daily touch with their parishioners and their problems. Together, the clinicians and clergymen probably have the most down-to-earth practical knowledge of mental and spiritual health in The Big Easy.

Visits to mental health clinics and churches have produced only such subjective impressions as the following, from the director of a clinic: "Sure, there are differences, but they're only what you would expect. People here drink a lot; hypertension is low because folks tend to act out their problems; and high blood pressure is more common among blacks than whites, as is usually the case." Big deal.

These various impressions were intriguing for one reason, however—their utter inconsistency. "New Orleanians have absolutely the same mental health problems as any other large American city," one priest claimed. "No better, no worse." "This place is an asylum without walls," declared a staffer from a clinic.

Obviously, then, multiple opinions must be sought, and from all the leading authorities. So our advisers drew up a long list of bonafide experts, people who are said to spend their days immersed in the diagnosis and treatment of mental disorders. A questionnaire was prepared; forms were duplicated. At last, science would either uphold or debunk The Big Easy theory.

But expert Number One was out fishing in Terrebonne Parish with expert Number Three when our interviewer called. Expert Number Two was not back from her weekend, while experts Four through Eight were all still at lunch when our interviewer showed up for his three o'clock meeting. Expert Number Nine was involved with an office party, which the interviewer joined, thus missing his scheduled meetings with experts Numbers Ten and Eleven, both of whom, meanwhile, had left messages saying that they left work early that day. Expert Number Twelve was at an emergency meeting of the St. Joseph's Day parade committee in his neighborhood, an urgent session that was called to decide whether the band should precede or follow the children with flowers.

Perhaps one day it will be possible to get a more definitive answer on whether New Orleans is really "The City That Care Forgot."

ENTICEMENT

In the depth of night when most Americans are sleeping, the big eighteen-wheel rigs are thundering across the interstates. In the Diamond T and Mack cabs there is music playing, more often than not the Dave Nemo Show from New Orleans. Beamed across the land by the clear-channel voice of the Jesuit-owned station WWL, the Dave Nemo Show keeps the old New Orleans myth alive.

The trucker is the keelboatman of today—brawny, lonely and sentimental. With country music, fast buck contests and reports on road and weather conditions for highways from Montana to Maine, the garrulous Dave Nemo entertains and cheers up the owner-operators between pit stops. After all, as the jingle says,

Every man is entitled to some help along the way,
And Trucker, you're more than a man...

The "help" may be a recording of Nemo's former colleague, Charlie Douglas, reciting his outrageous story of "The Talking Outhouse" or "The Mule Eggs." Or it might be the welcome news that someone in Fort Scott, Kansas, wants to hire drivers. Mostly it is just good cheer dished out, as Dave says, "from way down yonder in New Orleans."

It works. The proverbial letters and postcards flood into Dave Nemo's office on Rampart Street in the French Quarter. Many truckers drop through town just to say "Howdy." Even those who don't call are reminded by Nemo that New Orleans today, just as a century ago, is a kind of lighthouse and enticer to the lonely figure covering America's moonlit miles as everyone sleeps.

BUMMING

They came from Florida and Georgia, Rhode Island and Pennsylvania, Iowa and Arizona. Their jackets are torn at the shoulder seams and their shoes stiff and mud-caked from sun and rain. Their hair is shaggy and falls about the ears; their eyes, looking out through sun-bleached lashes, are swollen, watery, and red—the effects of exposure and drink.

Welcome to the Ozanam Inn, the Vincentian Brothers' hostel for bums on Camp Street.

The bland red brick building houses a cafeteria, a sedate lobby, and, up the iron steps, an ocean of beds, all turned down and ready for their occupants. Bibles, diet books, mild girly magazines, and copies of Toffler's *Future Shock* lie incongruously on the few night stands. Peeling plaster statues of Christ adorn each corner, His multiple arms embracing everyone in the room.

Business is brisk at the Ozanam Inn; twenty thousand free meals a month is the norm, with well over a million in the course of its short history. The stream of vagrants flows on and on, coming from every part of the country, and extending backward in time to the coming of the first Americans to New Orleans.

A short walk from the Ozanam Inn is Girod Street. In the old days it was a haven for flatboatmen and bums who went there to drink, gamble, brawl, and carouse. Young Abe Lincoln probably passed through "The Swamp," as it was called, when he hit town in 1825.

By the mid-nineteenth century, the center of low life had shifted eastward to Gallatin Street in the French Quarter, a particularly mean and sordid lane that has since been renamed French Market Place. A generation later the epicenter of vagrancy had moved to Basin Street, which is why they sang the blues there.

It is still shifting. Hard by the Ozanam Inn is one of the City's newest haute cuisine restaurants. Overnight, the neighborhood became far less appealing for low-budget dinners. Just as this was happening, representatives of a guru's sect showed up on Camp Street offering to "purchase" the City's bums for relocation in Oregon. Some event. Most are returning in quick order, however, no doubt upon the discovery that gurus don't eat muffalettas. With this conceptual breakthrough life goes back to normal.

Who are today's drifters? Some are boatmen and oil riggers temporarily on the outs. There also are family men among them, alcoholics, professional men, drug addicts, priests struck with wanderlust, and poets. Among the first guests at the Ozanam Inn on Palm Sunday, 1955, was a psychiatrist.

Like the tide, New Orleans draws such human flotsam and jetsam to itself, holds them briefly in its eddy, and then sweeps them on to more remote shores. The tide is endless.

THE SACRED AND THE PROFANE

*In which it is shown how
true piety can thrive in
unlikely zip codes,
like wheat among the tares.*

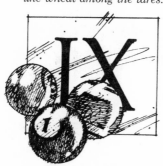

Standing offer

THE SACRED AND THE PROFANE

Few spots in New Orleans are more suffused with serene piety than the lovely garden on Royal Street behind the Cathedral. Rising above the ancient churchyard is a statue of Christ, His arms outstretched. Toward what? Toward Bourbon Street, its honky-tonk parade of tourists and tarts only a block from the Cathedral.

Nowhere in the United States do the sacred and the profane stand in closer relation to each other than in New Orleans. Puritan New England was created as the "City on a Hill," a community of anxious saints who left all worldliness behind them in England. Southern California blossomed as the very opposite, a suburb in the valley, a society freed from guilt, but with neither Heaven nor Hell to sustain it. New Orleans represents a third approach to life, richer and more textured than either, one in which the divine and the secular coexist and intermingle.

John James Audubon noticed this dimension of New Orleans in 1821 when he wrote of the sounds of Sunday in the Crescent City, with "church bells ringing and billiard balls knocking." Henry Fearon, another visitor of the same era, could hardly get over his astonishment at finding markets, shops, theaters, and ballrooms open on the Sabbath, along with the churches.

A cynic might argue that all this shows that the sacred is in full retreat on the lower Mississippi. Is there any other way to explain the following? For generations, the Catholic gentry of New Orleans has retired periodically for weekends of prayer at the white-columned Manrissa Retreat House, upriver from the city. It was long traditional to stop at a bar *en route* for a last toddy—until the Brothers bowed to the inevitable and began their retreat with a cocktail hour.

Then there is St. Joseph's Day, the festival of San Guiseppe, a Sicilian festival celebrated throughout southern Louisiana by stacking the altars high with mounds of the richest food. A few zealots still build their own home altars to St. Joseph, veritable mountains of edibles and potables. Our cynic would not fail to notice the fact that, coming on March 19, St. Joseph's Day provides a timely respite from fasting in the very midst of Lent.

The cynic will pile up further evidence to seal his case. He might speak of the Ursuline nun, Mother St. Croix, who sixty years ago devoted her days to the very this-worldly act of photography; of Sister Mary Blosl of the cloistered "Poor Claires," who is without doubt the greatest praline cook in Christendom and turns a handsome profit by selling her product extramurally; of the wakes in the Ninth Ward, with their amply stocked bars; or of the New Orleans funerals at which people begin dancing in the streets the moment the casket is in the tomb.

Guilty as charged? No. Those retreats are, for most, a genuine act of piety.

117

Mother St. Croix was renowned for her Christian humility and she lightly dismissed her work in photography; and Sister Mary, shrewd businesswoman that she is, began her praline industry in order to raise money for the starving Biafran peoples of Nigeria. And as to the wakes, should mourners starve?

Clearly, not all of the devout are ascetics, just as not all ascetics are devout. As *Ecclesiastes* puts it, "I know that there is nothing better for the sons of man than to be happy and to enjoy themselves as long as they live."

CLEAN-UP

In 1728 Sister Madeleine Hachard was sent to New Orleans to join the Ursulines there. Within very little time she had sized up the situation:

> ...the women of New Orleans are careless of their salvation, but not of their vanity...the greater part of them live on hominy but are dressed in velvet or damask trimmed with ribbons...The Devil has a vast empire here...

As living proof that Sister Madeleine's words applied also to the men, a Spanish immigrant, Antonio Ventura Carrion, reported in 1797 his own view that "In this life one must eat, drink, and enjoy oneself, because after death there is nothing." On the basis of his residence in New Orleans, Carrion claimed that this was the philosophy of life of everyone in Louisiana.

It is scarcely news to report that New Orleans is partly under the jurisdiction of the devil's empire. What is less appreciated are the innumerable efforts over the centuries to bring down his satanic regime. Short of the neutron bomb, virtually every weapon has been employed.

The assault on evil began in the 1730's, when New Orleans reprobates could be broken on the wheel. Later, the Spanish governor Don Alexander O'Reilly proposed surgery: "Who shall revile our Savior or His Mother, the Holy Virgin Mary, shall have his tongue cut out..."

By far the most efficient mechanism for stamping out bigamy and otherwise assuring that laymen and clergy toed the moral line was the "Holy Office of the Inquisition." These were the folks who organized public bonfires in Spain, and they tried to clean up the Crescent City as well.

The Inquisition established itself officially in the French Quarter in 1786. In addition to its usual targets, the New Orleans office was particularly concerned with dirty books, which in 1786 meant tracts by Voltaire and Rousseau. Porno movies and T-shirt shops had yet to make their appearances, of course.

Surprisingly, New Orleanians rather liked their "Ecclesiastical Judge," Antonio De Sedella, or "Pere Antoine" as the Creoles called him. Pere Antoine had his work cut out for him. He soon realized that he needed to be able to call on the *Corps de Garde* "at any hour of the night," a request that the Spanish Governor viewed with high skepticism.

For all his good intentions, Pere Antoine failed. The reason? Because, as the local Spanish bureaucrats understood, if de Sedella did his work too thoroughly it would eventually hurt trade, which New Orleans could ill afford. Eventually this foe of Satan was discreetly reassigned elsewhere. This was not to be the last clean-up campaign thwarted by tradesmen and the tourist industry.

Half a century after the Inquisition closed its branch in the French Quarter, America's greatest bard, Walt Whitman, was in the Big Easy living on Washington Street near the Mississippi River. In Whitman's eyes, New Orleans was "this goodly city...(albeit not so very good, either)." It all sounds so familiar.

ORIGINAL SIN

Heaven has only one entrance, but many of New Orleans' older restaurants had two: one for just about everyone, and the other for gentlemen who were entertaining women with whom they did not want to be seen in public. At Commander's Palace the second door still exists, discreetly around the corner from the main entrance. It is locked nowadays, as are the old private rooms at Antoine's.

Such a gentleman on the town might have begun his evening at the French Opera on Bourbon Street. There he and his "guest" could watch *La Sonnambula* while sitting demurely behind the latticed front of a *loge grille*, unseen by the public and by his wife.

Surveying such practices, the Mississippi-born novelist Walker Percy characterized New Orleans as

...A kind of comfortable Catholic limbo somewhere between the

119

outer circle of Hell, where sexual sinners don't have it all that bad,
and the inner circle of purgatory, where things are even better.

But there is no point in dwelling upon such antique practices. They are extinct today—anyone can confirm that—and New Orleans did not invent the double standard anyway. The one aspect of such behavior in New Orleans that is noteworthy is the extent to which in the old days it was institutionalized. The system expected it and adjusted to it.

Which is how Storyville came into being in 1897. For two decades, New Orleans' City Council in effect legalized prostitution, and lent it the support of law within a twenty-block area. The aldermen presumably reasoned that human nature is weak and that prostitution and other evils are bound to exist, so why kid ourselves? Live and let live.

Philip Freneau, the poet who celebrated the American Revolution, predicated that

Men will rise from what they are;
sublimer and superior, far...

New Orleans stands in a different tradition, less striving, less optimistic, less anxious over present realities. In short, it has come to terms with Original Sin. That is why the lyrics of the 1922 hit "Way Down Yonder in New Orleans" are dead wrong when they call the city "a garden of Eden." Forbidden fruit is a regular part of the local diet—not for all inhabitants of New Orleans, of course, but for enough to set the tone.

To err is human, to forgive divine. New Orleanians revel in the exercise of divinity. When several local businessmen were convicted of malfeasance and were to be jailed, their friends threw a rousing party for them on the eve of their departure. "Sure they made a mistake," the hosts acknowledged, "but they are paying their debt, so why punish them further?"

In another city they would probably have been ostracized—a more "sublime and superior" response, to be sure, but not necessarily a more human one. Such are the choices people make.

PIETY

Is it significant that Desire Street and Piety Street in New Orleans run parallel to each other, and are only yards apart? That Desire is a two-way thoroughfare while Piety can be traversed in only one direction? Or that Desire gets most of the traffic, leaving Piety a peaceful byway?

Those who conceive of New Orleans only as a fleshpot with five-star restaurants might find all this pregnant with meaning. But study this heavily black neighborhood more closely. You will soon discover far more piety than desire. Indeed piety blooms in the very heart of Desire, at number 1230, to be exact. There stands the Greater Liberty Baptist Church. There are far more church pews than bar stools in New Orleans, and a visit to Greater Liberty reveals why.

Every service is rich with music. The choir, under the direction of Ceola Cherrie, is well-rehearsed, its voices lavish and strong. The arrangements are nearly all original, for that is part of Ms. Cherrie's job, just as it was part of Bach's duties to arrange music each week for the choir of the St. Thomas Church in Leipzig. Yet this is not what accounts for the splendor of the singing at Greater Liberty. Rather, it is the overwhelming spiritual heat that the music conveys. This special intensity is not to be found in any secular ensemble or jazz band in New Orleans, both of which seem pallid and mechanical by comparison.

"People believe what they sing," wrote Alexander Solzhenitsyn. By this measure, New Orleans congregations are rocks of devotion, for they sing with an awesome spiritual fire. To hear the choir at St. Luke's African Methodist Episcopal Church plunge into "The Beatitude" in 6/8 time or to hear the integrated choir at St. Francis de Sales Catholic Church "sing the Mass" is to understand why the Old Testament psalmists were always singing.

The luxuriant growth of religious music in New Orleans is only part of the evidence of local piety. Letters to the editors of the local papers reflect it, as do published ads from the lovelorn, many of whom specify that they are seeking a religiously inclined mate. Church life spreads far beyond Sunday, filling evenings and weekends for many. Parishioners, even in poor neighborhoods, give generously to their church or temple. Several radio stations offer sermons and gospel hymns to sinner and repenter alike. Monastic orders continue to attract novices, both white and black, including not a few veterans of the Bourbon Street scene.

Is it not strange, then, that a New Orleanian has yet to make any significant contribution to the study of theology? Some great Catholic bishops came from the Crescent City but they made their mark as organizers, not thinkers. Walker Percy is the one deeply religious writer associated with the city, but his genius was formed not in New Orleans but in the Delta country of Mississippi—the same land of uneasy metaphysical souls that produced William Faulkner.

Perhaps it is because theological speculation is an activity of people whose faith is in transition, whether from ordeal or discovery. The devout of New Orleans are less inclined to speculate than to celebrate. This is certainly the case with Barbara Williams, a secretary who, at forty-two, is celebrating her first quarter-century as solo soprano with the choir at the Louisa Street Baptist Church. She is ebullient and hearty, a stranger both to puritanism and religious doubt. When Barbara Williams sings, the handkerchiefs come out and the New Testament lives.

ARISTOCRATS

*In which it is shown that the local ethnic pot
simmers rather than boils,
leading to a lumpy gumbo
rather than mush.*

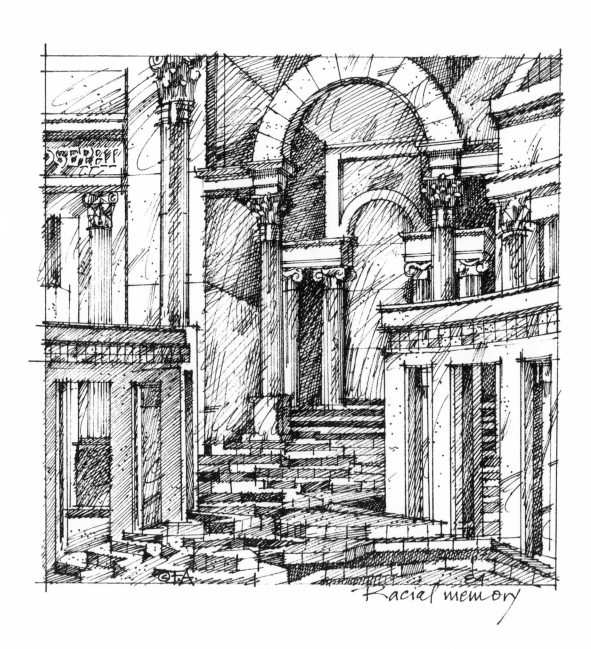

Racial memory

126

ARISTOCRATS

It was 1954, the year of the historic *Brown vs. Board of Education* case and the twilight of legal segregation in New Orleans. Late that spring the *Louisiana Weekly* reported that "a group of charming ladies met under the fig tree in Mrs. (Sorina) Synigal's patio." After tea and cakes, the ladies announced the establishment of *La Creole Fete Association de la Nouvelle Orleans*. Over the next decades, the *Fete* would organize historical tours, render social services, and hold elegant balls at the St. Mary of the Angels gym. Invitations advised *"mesdames et mademoiselles"* to wear long gowns. Those participating in *La Creole Fete* had—and have—names like Meullier, Montegut, Duplessis, Dugue, Breaux, and Damesilliere.

These people, still central to the life of New Orleans, are black Creoles. Descended from French-Negro mixing, they bear French names, adhere to the Catholic faith, and have an almost proprietary sense of belonging. They have every right to. Of all the many groups in New Orleans' population, they are the only one compounded wholly on the spot. The city created them.

And they helped create the city. By 1770 Negroes were already buying their freedom in New Orleans. Many other free Negroes emigrated to New Orleans from Santo Domingo around 1800, bringing their considerable property with them. Over the next half-century the Crescent City came to boast the largest free black population of any North American metropolis, including New York. *Gens de couleur libres,* or "free people of color," were property-owners, builders, tradesmen, artists, planters, and even slaveholders. Some of them went abroad to France for study. In New Orleans they formed their own symphony orchestra in 1838 and 1845 they published a French language literary collection, *Les Cenelles (Holly Berries)* that still makes interesting reading. A rich cultural life suffused the community, embracing young and old alike. For as Camille Thierry wrote:

> *De tout barde creole*
> *Une jeune beauté*
> *Reclamé un chant frivolé*
> *Ou triste `a volonte.*

> (From every Creole bard
> A young beauty
> Demands a song, frivolous
> Or sad, it makes no difference.)

The poetry ceased after the War Between the States as black Creoles saw their position erode. Anglo-Saxon New Orleans, unlike the old French city, had difficulty finding a place for men and women who were both black and, in many cases, well educated. But the worthiness of the black Creole leadership was never in doubt. And the Creole blacks, in contrast to their white Creole counterparts, did not lose ground to the "American" immigrants of their own race.

Today, descendents of the "free people of color" are more prominent in local life than ever before. The one real change that has occurred is that the old prejudices that held Creole blacks aloof from the rest of the black population are nearly gone. One of their number, Ernest N. Morial, has been popularly elected to two terms as mayor. A recent election produced a crop of capable black Creole candidates, men named Valteau, Boissier, Julien, and the like. There are non-Creole black politicians too, of course, but to be black and Creole is still to have a leg up in New Orleans.

SEMITISM

New Orleans is home to proportionately one of the largest and most civic-minded Jewish populations in North America. They play a central role in the city's life. Never mind that Jews have been excluded from a few clubs and societies, for so has most everyone else. Never mind, also, that no Jew has ever served as mayor of the Crescent City, for no Protestant has attained that honor either. What counts is that Jewish leadership is crucial to many important institutions in the Crescent City. Compared with this, even the absence of a good Jewish delicatessen here pales to insignificance.

The important place of Jews in New Orleans can be traced to a corpulent man who was once compelled to flee the country disguised as a cook. The man in question was Judah P. Benjamin, identified by the *Encyclopedia Judaica* as "undoubtedly the most prominent nineteenth-century American Jew." During the three decades before the Civil War, Benjamin, who attended Yale, established himself as the leading lawyer in New Orleans. A successful sugar planter as well, his plantations gave him the means to pursue a career in public life. His fellow Louisianans elected him to the U.S. Senate in 1852, the first professing Jew to sit in that chamber. He would have been the first Jew on the Supreme Court as well, but he turned down the appointment.

Fiercely loyal to his city and state, Benjamin resigned from the Senate as soon as

Louisiana seceded from the Union. During the next four years he acted as a one-man brain trust for the Confederacy. First as Attorney General, then as Secretary of War, and finally as Secretary of State, he did his best to buoy up the Lost Cause. Then he fled to England.

It was not long before Benjamin was recognized as one of the most prominent barristers in London. He became Queen's Counsel to Victoria and wrote a textbook on the law of sales that is still the standard authority on the subject.

Not bad for a Jewish boy from downtown! And Benjamin was not one of those Jews who made it to the top by denying his heritage. When a fellow member of the U.S. Senate directed an anti-Semitic quip towards him, Benjamin took the podium to caution that:

> The gentleman will please remember that when his half-civilized ancestors were hunting wild boars in the forests of Silesia, mine were Princes of the Realm of Solomon.

His practical skills, his awesome legal mind, and not least of all his rich sense of humor endeared Benjamin to all who met him. New Orleans lawyers still bow before his memory.

The prestige of the Queen's Counsel doubtless paved the way for another Jew, Louis Salomon, to be chosen the first Rex of Mardi Gras in 1872. Other offices followed, less regal, to be sure, but close to the city's heartbeat nonetheless.

WOP SALAD

If you are over six feet tall and carry life insurance, here is a sociological experiment to be performed *seriatim* in San Francisco, South Philadelphia, and New Orleans. First, find a typical local Italian restaurant. Then walk in and let them seat you, preferably near the door. When the waiter comes to take your order, smile amiably and ask for "Wop Salad."

In almost any self-respecting Italian community in the United States, your order will unleash a fury unmatched since the Romans dismantled Carthage. Plates will fly and rococo oaths will fill the air. Your dentist will soon be able to buy that new Mercedes he's been eyeing.

But a Mandina's, Mandich's, Campagno's or any of a dozen other fine Italian restaurants in New Orleans, the experiment will turn out differently. Your waiter will respond to your order by inquiring what dressing you want and whether or not you want a Dixie with your Wop Salad. For in New Orleans, Wop Salad is just a name. If you hadn't ordered it yourself, the waiter might have suggested it with a Sicilian twinkle, and you would be foolish to ignore his advice.

"Aha!" you say. Here is that rare case of happy and uneventful assimilation, a rags-to-riches success story that leaves its heroes full of benign humor and good will! But it was by no means so simple for New Orleans' Italians. Most of them arrived in Louisiana virtually as indentured servants, brought there to take the place of departing Negroes in the sugarcane fields.

Things must have been pretty bad around Palermo for such a life to look appealing. But the immigrants poured in by the thousands. They arrived with no money but they did bring their way of life, including annual fêtes on St. Rosalie's Day and St. Joseph's Day, and rich and distinctive cuisine. They also brought some well-aged vendettas with them, not to mention the Mafia, which surfaced in New Orleans prior to its debut in New York.

On the night of October 15, 1890, New Orleans' young, popular, and corrupt chief of police, David Hennessey, was murdered, apparently by members of a Sicilian gang. When the jury unexpectedly acquitted the accused, New Orleans vigilantes held a mass meeting on Canal Street and then marched on the municipal prison. Thirteen Italians were lynched. "Wop" became a very ugly word.

So once more, the Italians had to start over, and from the very bottom. This time they became more New Orleanian than the native New Orleanians themselves. They lived in poor neighborhoods and among blacks, which accounts for the large number of Sicilian boys among the pioneer generation of jazzmen. In fact, the first jazz record, issued twenty-seven years after the lynching, featured the Original Dixieland Jass (sic.) Band, led by trumpeter Nick LaRocca, the son of an immigrant shoemaker from Sicily. With his epochal recording of 1917, LaRocca became a standard-bearer for the entire city.

Italians made it back. They distinguished themselves in the professions, in government, in business, in education. Today the boldest contemporary architecture in New Orleans is the "Piazza d'Italia," built by the proud Italian community on sleek Poydras Street. It is an exuberant and unabashedly sentimental celebration of all that is florid in Italy, the very qualities that earlier kept Sicilian immigrants at arm's length from Anglo-Saxon society.

Wop Salad is the culinary version of the Piazza d'Italia. It is the product of confident people who view their history with nostalgia and good-natured pride rather than bitterness.

Eventually, the Mafia made it back, too, but this time by invitation rather than through intrigue. It seems that around the year 1935 U.S. Senator Huey Long approached gangland boss Frank Costello in New York, requesting that Costello-owned slot machines be placed in the New Orleans area. The "Kingfish," in collaboration with local bigwigs, offered to provide protection for the operation in exchange for a large cut of the profits—which he planned to spend on the widows and orphans of the Pelican State.

Costello, sensing rightly that Huey was his kind of man, accepted the proposal. This time there were no vigilantes, at least not until a local doctor gunned down the Kingfish in a marble hall of the new capitol in Baton Rouge.

LATINS

New Orleans has waxed prosperous through its contact with the North, but not without problems. New Orleans' wealth has also grown through its links with the Caribbean world to the South, but without most of the difficulties. Today this situation is changing, as the Latin American trade shifts to Houston and Miami and as new problems arise from illegal traffic in drugs. But for most of its history, the Crescent City was the northernmost outpost of the Caribbean world, and a very successful one at that—which is why the existing French Quarter and Jackson Square are more Spanish than French.

Travel timetables and ticket prices tell the whole story. From New Orleans, it is far cheaper to fly to Mexico City than to New York. Havana and Haiti are far easier to reach by boat than are Baltimore or Cincinnati. And in the old days, if you sailed to Europe from New Orleans, your ship would call in at least one Caribbean port. In fact, most contacts between New Orleans and France passed through the Caribbean filter. It is small wonder that thousands of fine old Creole families, both white and black, trace their ancestry to aristocrats and *gens de couleur libres* who emigrated to New Orleans by the thousands from Haiti (Santo Domingo) after a slave revolt there in 1791. New Orleans, after all, was a Caribbean capital.

The Crescent City has absorbed much from Latin life. The "tango belt" that flourished on the Lake side of the French Quarter in the early years of this century, the hot tamales that are still sold on street corners, the fireworks on New Year's Eve—all bespeak this influence, which can also be detected in the deliciously rich music of New Orleans composer Louis Moreau Gottschalk, who lived in the Caribbean, of Jelly Roll Morton, and of the rhythm-and-blues genius, James

Booker.

The attraction between New Orleans and the Caribbean is mutual. The Crescent City is well-established as a playground for the elite of Central and South America, a shopping center for the good life. With careful planning, a visiting businessman from Caracas or Bogota can shop for the family, get his annual checkup at the fine Ochsner Clinic, and visit his mistress in New Orleans, all on one trip. That such a maneuver entails certain risks only adds to the pleasure of it all.

CONVERTS

New Orleans, like America as a whole, is populated by immigrants. French were among the first to come, then Germans, Africans, Spanish, Anglo-Saxons, Carribean Creoles, Irish, Croatians, Italians, and most recently Vietnamese and Latin Americans. Throughout the 1800's about half the population was foreign-born. The percentage is still high today.

How then, can one possibly speak of any "tradition" being transmitted by so fluid a populace? It is possible in part because each group remakes the city in its own image, and then that revised image over time comes to stand for the city as a whole. The Anglo-Saxons who built the Garden District were immigrants, both from elsewhere in the United States and from abroad, just as the Italians would later be. And Mahalia Jackson, the incomparable gospel singer, grew up in a neighborhood of rural black immigrants who settled in the Carrollton area. The glory of New Orleans society is to have allowed itself to be changed by such immigrants, and even to be defined by them.

At the very time the city is being changed by the immigrant's presence, however, New Orleans reshapes the immigrant in return. For example, few Chinese found their way to the Crescent City until recent years. But by the 1950's a hearty band of them were participating in Mardi Gras activities by forming their own Krewe of the Golden Dragon. In addition to being Americanized, they were New Orleanated.

This process has been continual from the start. German settlers with names like Zweig became LaBranche, Weber became Fabre, and Jake Schneider became Schexnaydre. The Irish-born architect, James Gallagher, emerged in New Orleans as Gallier; many people today assume he was Creole.

Strange to say, Mardi Gras itself was organized in its modern form not by scions of old Creole families but by the more recently arrived Anglo-Saxons. New Orleanated Protestants, full of enthusiasm for their new home, also took up the French Catholic celebration of All Saints Day, in spite of the fact that some of their anti-Roman denominations had been created in protest against the veneration of the saints.

Because New Orleans' black community lived so settled an existence from the earliest days, it was especially adept at assimilating newcomers. What were jazzmen Joe ("King") Oliver or Edward ("Kid") Ory like before their arrival in the Crescent City from Aben and LaPlace, Louisiana? No one knows, so quickly did they merge with the life of their adopted home.

One reason New Orleans continues to be New Orleans is that most of those who choose to move there are precisely the ones most likely to adapt easily once there. The city's new Chinese come largely from freewheeling Canton and Hong Kong rather than from the more austere north of China. Nearly all New Orleans' Italians come from the kindred environment of Sicily. Recent Russian-Jewish immigrants hail mainly from Odessa, the most Mediterranean of Soviet cities and, with its French origins and its traditions of improvised band music, a kind of soul mate to New Orleans. Through self-selection, immigrants to New Orleans tend to be those who, even in their place of origin, were already partly New Orleanians in spirit.

Will this continue? Will New Orleans be able for long to refashion its new citizens in its own image? Or will America's mono-culture take over, swamping all indigenous life or permitting it to continue only as a plasticized caricature of itself?

It is far too early to say, of course. But it may be pertinent to note that back in 1803, Creole New Orleanians were asking precisely the same question. They feared that hard-driving Yankees would turn their city into a tropical Philadelphia, a perspiring Boston. They need not have worried.

PIGEON-HOLES

Just how New Orleanians spent the day of July 4, 1776, is lost in the primordial humidity. In all likelihood, they ate, worked from ten to two and then ate some more, mopping their brows all the while. Certainly they did not spend the day as those worthies in Philadelphia did, affirming that all men are created equal. The very idea was absurd, and dangerous besides, for when the Inquisition came to New Orleans it had made it clear that it had no use for the notion of equality.

This does not mean that the Crescent City is organized into hierarchical classes— for classes imply a society shaped like one of those tiered pyramids of ancient Egypt. When you climb upward from one step, you inevitably arrive at a new step, which finally culminates in one single point at the pinnacle. New Orleans' social life is compartmentalized, to be sure. But its overall configuration is more comparable to a symphony orchestra than to a pyramid. The second flautist struggles like mad to become first flute; but once there he does not aspire to become a violinist, which is clearly impossible. Instead, he strains to solidify his position in the flute section, and then to make sure the orchestra as a whole plays music filled with solos for flute.

This helps explain the Homeric wrath of Mr. Wayne Crozier, aged 34, against the Mystic Krewe of Shangri-La down in the suburb of Chalmette. Crozier, it seems, paid several thousand dollars to the ladies of Chalmette for the honor of reigning as king of their six hundred-member Carnival krewe. Then Crozier's wife got into a tiff with a Shangri-La officer and Crozier was asked to abdicate. Immediately he went looking for Shangri-La's captain, Mrs. Mary Lopatio. He found her behind the counter at her dog grooming shop. When Crozier asked for his money back, Mrs. Lopatio refused. So he sued for $100,000.

Why didn't Crozier just tell off Mary Lopatio and look for a more high-toned krewe with which to celebrate Mardi Gras? In other words, why didn't he thumb his nose at Shangri-La and climb up the social ladder to a level at which he and Mrs. Crozier would be appreciated? He didn't, and for the same reason that the flautist does not move to the violin section. Crozier belonged where he was and knew he had no claim to a position higher up. But he could insist on getting his due within his assigned sphere. This is just what Wayne Crozier did.

The negative aspects of New Orleans' special brand of social pigeon-holing are obvious. All too often careers really are not open to talent. Good people often leave the city rather than face what they see as insurmountable barriers to their professional advancement. On the other hand, if you accept the terms of this unusual social compact, you are rewarded with a nice sense of belonging. For each compartment is a fully-equipped micro-society in itself, with organizations and institutions similar to those in every other compartment, but scaled down or up to fit the means and circumstances of the particular group. By participating in the life of your compartment, you participate in the whole. Hence the forty different Mardi Gras krewes and balls, and the scores of different civic clubs. Hence, too, the civic pride that pervades the population to a depth that would be unthinkable in more democratically constituted cities.

In this connection, it is worth recalling the Mardi Gras of 1913. Few actually remember it, of course, but many New Orleanians know of it, for such knowledge is as commonplace here as the mastery of baseball trivia elsewhere. In that year, the Rex organization chose the theme of "Utopia." The floats dealt with such fanciful and absurd themes as "Where Butterflies Draw Chariots." Imagine such a notion! And right after the butterfly float came another, equally fanciful, entitled "Where All Men Are Equal."

FRAGMENTS

Just about everyone has a niche somewhere in the gothic confusion of New Orleans' social structure. More accurately, just about everyone's *group* does, thanks to which the individual derives his or her place among the gargoyles. Depending on how a person views his assigned group and what aspirations he or she may have beyond it, and depending also on whether one likes the architecture of the structure as a whole, the situation can be comforting, or very frustrating—or both.

For all its internal complexity, this structure barely extends beyond the Orleans Parish line. Viewed from just a few miles out, the social edifice looks like the intricate towers of a French cathedral rising out of the green plain. Far out on that plain (and in South Louisiana, in the marshes beyond), neither the benefits nor the drawbacks of urban society are felt. Many and diverse groups of people are to be found out there, but they do not fit neatly into any larger structure locally. They remain like building blocks for some monument that was never constructed.

One such group are the Isleños, a few thousand Spaniards from the Canary Islands who dwell amidst the lacey web of bayous and lagoons that fans out to the south and east of New Orleans in St. Bernard Parish. Only minutes from the city, the Isleños inhabit another world. Their antique dialect of Spanish dates to the eighteenth century, when the King of Spain sent the first Canary Islanders to the New Orleans area to fend off possible British raids on the colony.

Isleno Spanish has slipped to the status of a second language in recent years, for the trappers and fishermen of St. Bernard no longer pull their children out of school between December and February each year in order to work the marshes. But there are still Isleños who can recite *decimas*, Hispanic epic poems dating back four centuries and more. Just a few years ago José Campo, aged eighty, declaimed *"La Mora y la Mosca"* ("The Moorish Girl and the Fly") before a group of wide-eyed professors of linguistics at his house down in Chalmette.

Imagine the scene: a white-haired patriarch living on the very outskirts of New Orleans holding forth in a quaint dialect of Spanish about a Moorish lass who lived on another continent half a millenium ago...At a distance of barely a mile, and scarcely beyond earshot of the intent professors, one of the largest aluminum plants in the world thunders away, its thousands of employees caring not a whit about the Islamic girl, the fly, or Mr. Campo, for the matter. Their car radios are tuned to a different society, and so are they.

Which is not to say that Mr. Campo or his progeny feel particularly deprived. He and many other Islēnos are bothered by something quite different. They feel themselves part of a structure of human relations that centers not in New Orleans but far out in the Atlantic Ocean, on the Canary Islands. It is a distant world, and one that has all but forgotten that they are here.

MALES, ETC.

In which, through mutual concessions,
The Battle of the Sexes
gives way to a fragile detente,
albeit with
occasional skirmishes along the DMZ.

The Boston Club: Mission Control Canal

140

MALES

There are arts of building and arts of surviving. For two generations, until the gentlemen of OPEC turned everything upside down, New Orleans' men survived. Atlanta, Dallas, and Houston were racing ahead while New Orleans slipped badly. Outside interests bought out its industries, other local institutions dropped out of the big leagues, and its athletic teams barely got in. Those were bad days for local boosters and for local male leadership (which were practically the same).

How did the men of New Orleans respond? Some observers say they retreated into boys' games. Men who elswhere might be captains of industry devoted their energies to mounting baroque *tableaux* and running the social season. Losing ground to outside entrepreneurs, they picked up yardage even at the expense of women. One local country club went so far as to require that if a daughter inherited voting stock in it, her husband would have to join or she would forfeit her rights.

Confronting the larger crisis from a position of weakness, New Orleans' male leaders tried valiantly to make a common stand, to keep their own ranks united. In their dealings with one another they avoided face-to-face conflict, preferring behind-the-scenes negotiations wherever possible. Rather than offer a firm "No" to what might be a ridiculous business proposition from an old friend, the standard method was to nod gravely and equivocably, waffle for a few weeks and then do nothing. Everyone understands. In their societies and organizations they gave inordinate power to the blackball, the surest guarantor of conformism. Strange chains of clientage developed, having more in common with Meiji Japan than with the United States. Those placed lower on such chains meekly refrained from taking any actions until they knew how those placed at the top of the chain would act. This kept the ranks intact, heaven knows, but it also institutionalized weakness and dependence. And it made the gents sitting ducks for opportunists from elsewhere.

At this point all John Wayne fans and other devotees of hot-blooded dynamism can stop reading. By their standards, the male survivors of New Orleans just don't pack the gear. They can be ignored.

But those same men possess other virtues that are unknown to the *macho* crowd of hyperactive doers. They have the time of day for friendships. They are reserved, but hospitable to a fault. Being acutely aware of their own failings, they are quick to forgive the weaknesses of others. Their sense of humor is genuine and honed by constant exercise. And for the most part, they are excellent family men. The exceptions only prove the rule.

The New Orleans old guard is no more given to philosophizing than to action. If it were, its motto might be: "If you win a rat race, you're still a rat."

141

The rarity of this attitude in the mainstream of male American Babbittry shows once more that not all desirable ends in this life are compatible.

POKER

Some months ago an admiring New Orleans reporter bestowed the ultimate compliment on Louisiana's Senator Russell Long: "Long shows the value of playing his political cards close to his chest and avoiding commitments until the last possible minute."

A New Orleans lady, genteel and definitely not a card shark, publicly advised the Mayor on a local issue: "He [the Mayor] is playing political poker...Let's request that the Mayor pool his chips."

Up in the Boston-Washington corridor, in Chicago, or in Los Angeles, the reigning metaphors for public life and politics are drawn from the argot of the stock market. Some might "sell short," "feel bullish" or engage in "profit taking." In New Orleans, by contrast, public life is a kind of poker game without the cards. One "ups the ante," has a "wild card," or exercises "dealer's choice." The 2,598,960 possible combinations of the five-card hand embrace every conceivable variant of the human condition.

Poker is to New Orleans as waltzing is to Vienna, firecrackers to Beijing. In its modern form, it was born there. Actually the French brought the game of *Poque* with them to Louisiana, having earlier borrowed it from the German game of *Pochen* (meaning "to bluff"), which in turn came from the English game *Brag*. Americans quickly took it up, anglicized the name to "poker," and invented the 52-card deck. By the 1830's, riverboat gamblers had spread the game throughout the West.

Poker, which has enriched New Orleans life for a century and a half, is as vigorously pursued today as ever in the past. Buddy Roemer, a U.S. Congressman from a neighboring district in south Louisiana, uses it to supplement his salary up in Washington. In one year he relieved Capitol Hill rubes of some $15,000. Asked by *Newsweek* about his passion for Louisiana-style cutthroat poker, Roemer explained, "It's my hobby."

Why did *Poque* take hold, and why do New Orleanians still perceive the world through its lens? Because poker rewards *human* skills, not just technical proficiency. And of the human skills that poker demands, none is more important

142

than the ability to bluff and to detect when others are bluffing. In a place where the powerful can be poor and the poor can be powerful, bluff is everything. The successful bluff can turn nothing into something or it can give the appearance of something when there is nothing. The bluff unmasked is power lost; to the one who unmasks it, power gained. Poker is the most secretive of games and New Orleans is the most secretive of cities.

No wonder the late New Orleans judge, Oliver Carriere, is said to have held that "the way a man behaves in a poker game is the way he behaves in life."

PESSIMISM

New Orleans' Moisant Field is named for a pioneer aviator who crashed.

Gravier Street, the old business center of the city, is named for a real estate speculator who went broke.

Sometimes one senses that success in New Orleans is transitory and only failure is permanent. Paraphrasing Tolstoy, all successes here seem the same, while each tale of failure is unique and endlessly intriguing. The richest man in nineteenth-century New Orleans, Bernard Xavier Philipe de Marigny de Mandeville, ended his days a pauper but has a *faubourg* named for him. There are new Marignys today, hugely successful, but they may not be memorialized until they, too, have passed beyond the transitory stage of success.

ELOCUTION

If the South has produced anything in both Grade A quality and prodigious quantity, it is orators. Any crossroad town in Alabama or Georgia has its own arm-waving, brow-mopping, tub-thumping master of rhetoric, the man whose silver tongue can bulldoze any argument his opponents can throw against him. To contain such fountains of eloquence, a South Carolinian, Henry Robert, penned his *Robert's Rules of Order,* wherein strict procedures on cloture are spelled out. Other Southerners responded to Robert by inventing the filibuster.

New Orleans stands outside this tradition. Very few great orators cut their teeth here and those who did—men like Judah P. Benjamin or Bishop Leonidas Polk—are instantly recognizable as expectations. The local barristers affect a different style: they are slow to speak, deliberate, almost fumbling, and infinitely shrewd. The politicians, too, try to gain their ends through patient jawboning rather than oratory. When given the choice, they would rather cut deals in the corridors than capers on the stump.

True southern grandiloquence is nurtured best in the shadow of a Protestant pulpit. The Southern Baptists alone have produced more window-rattling expositors than the entire Athenian Republic at the time of Demosthenes. Add the Methodists and Prsbyterians and you have a phalanx that would leave Cicero groping for words.

Because of New Orleans' Catholic heritage, far fewer of its citizens are exposed to spread-eagle Bible-slapping oratory than would be the case in Atlanta or Dallas. The Latin mass, after all, does not quite invite the priest to engage in passionate verbal improvisation. No wonder, then, that many of Louisiana's most renowned spellbinders, Huey Long included, hail from the Protestant north of the state.

New Orleanians may not be great devotees of oratory, but they excel in one field of elocution—joke telling. Rare is the business meeting or social event that is not punctuated by at least one anecdote. At a recent funeral, a friend made his way gravely through the crowd of mourners to pass on one he had just heard while standing within feet of the casket. As usual, he told the story deadpan, underscoring the punch line only by the added measure of seriousness with which it was uttered. Then he looked thoughtfully off into space as the kicker sunk in. Before the funeral was over, half a dozen or more people had heard the joke and were spreading their own variations on it.

Where do New Orleanians get their jokes? Before the computerization of the stock market, jokes flew from city to city over the telegraph lines during lulls when the operators were not transmitting stock prices. When IBM closed down this channel, New Orleanians were thrown back on their own resources, which turned out to be formidable. Homegrown howlers proliferated and even became an export item, thanks to bartenders who pass them on to tourists. Then too, bawdy tales have always drifted into town from across the country in much the same way that the sewage of Little Falls, Minnesota, and McKeesport, Pennsylvania, eventually reaches the levee at Jackson Square.

The jokes themselves come in all flavors. In the bad old days before desegregation, the infamous Rastus tales were common among whites, and so were ethnic jokes directed against Italians, French, Yugoslavs, and Yankees. All this is thankfully in the past. The reigning butt of Crescent City humor today is the Cajun population, the French-speaking descendants of the Acadians from Nova Scotia who inhabit the bayou parishes west and south of New Orleans.

The adventures of Maurice and Mathilde are invariably ribald and their rural dialect a worthy challenge to any urban *raconteur*. Thanks to Mr. Justin Wilson of Denham Springs, Louisiana, it is possible to present a Cajun story that is both typical and printable. Here it is:

> *You know dey got a school in Sout' Lewisana where de teachin' lady ast a li'l boy name Placide, "What did Davy Crockett kill hisse'f, hanh?"*
> *An' Placide say like dis, "He kilt hisse'f a Cajun."*
> *"Dat don't ra't," de teacher say. "He kilt hisse'f a bear."*
> *An' Placide say real hot on de collar, "Well, if Hebert don't be a Cajun, w'at he are?"*

Justin Wilson and Howard Jacobs,
Justin Wilson's Cajun Humor,
Pelican Publishing Co., Gretna,
1979, p. 90.

FEMALES

New Orleans women have it rough. On the job they receive less pay for the same work than their counterparts elsewhere. Until recently, inheritance laws under Louisiana's French-type *Code Civil* kept women away from the family checkbook. New Orleans men even exercise control over the rituals surrounding the debutantes' world, elsewhere the domain of the ladies.

The liabilities extend into public life. Politics is still largely a male sport, like crap shooting. Outside of the cultural organizations, the few women on boards are all too often treated with gracious condescension. As to the Equal Rights Amendment—forget it. Its supporters were fewer than local contributors to the Albanian Relief Fund.

Is this because New Orleans men consider women to be naive and flighty bubbleheads? Not at all. On this point New Orleans males are absolutely unified, as they have been for centuries. To the extent that men exclude women from civic life, it is out of the deepest respect for their potential power. As a columnist for *The Times-Picayune* put it over a century ago, "The influence of women, if exerted without restraint, would result in the utter ruin of a community."

The writer, Lafcadio Hearn, understood the power that women in New Orleans can wield. When the Union Army occupied this Confederate city, the men lay low, biding their time until better days arrived. But not so the women, as Lincoln's local potentate, General "Spoons" Butler, learned to his indignation. When New Orleans women passed Butler's officers on the street, they snubbed them, even spat upon them. Butler was not amused.

It is unlikely that such manifestations of principle surprised anyone. As early as 1808 a visitor to the city, Thomas Ashe, observed that "the women...in point of manners and character have a very marked superiority over the men." Ashe referred specifically to "women of both ranks—the white and the brown."

Because they have not been co-opted into the system, New Orleans women feel less constrained to observe its niceties. They march in where males fear to tread. Back in the twenties the French Quarter was eminently *déclassé*, neglected by the conformist menfolk. But a group of women organized themselves into a new club, the "Petit Salon," and set about the task of restoring it. Later, women earned general's rank in the wars for historic preservation.

White and black, Christian and Jewish, it is primarily the women who have built up and maintained New Orleans' cultural life. They have received dignitaries from abroad in their homes, charged the churches with energy, and stood behind the symphony, opera, and ballet companies.

The beginning of wisdom in politics is to be able to distinguish between form and substance, the appearance of power and true muscle. On this issue the women of New Orleans could write the book.

FAMILIES

Go to a New Orleans shoe store and eavesdrop on the conversations around you. You will hear little about the merits of the shoes, even the fanciest ones. Instead, the salesmen and their customers will be discussing their respective families:

"You related to Eddie Boudreaux out on Marais Street?"

"Why, yes, he's my husband's uncle."

"Oh yeah? Why, Eddie's wife, Winona, is my wife's second cousin."

With this the sale is sealed. The customer has established the salesman's identity in the firmament of New Orleans. The salesman is no longer a stranger. And being practically family, would he dare pull a fast one on you?

New Orleans is a family town. Bank loans are made and stocks are traded on the same basis as the transaction at the shoe store. All this can happen when large numbers of families stay put in the same place. A survey of New Orleans high school graduates reveals that few leave town either for college or work—far fewer than in most American cities. This tendency leads to intermarriage and to family trees that look like botanical fantasies. Many family names, including certain Italian and Creole names rarely heard elsewhere, run on for whole columns in the New Orleans phone book. An older citizen who attended the Cathedral School in the 1920's recalls that only four children in his first grade class were not his cousins. The 125 members of the St. Luke's African Methodist Episcopal Church on Louisa Street all come from just five family chains.

The history of jazz in New Orleans is in good measure a history of families, for the cultivation of music is passed through the generations like an heirloom. The prolific Humphrey clan, now led by the clarinetist-patriarch, Willie, has spawned bandsmen for over a century, extending backwards in time to the Magnolia Plantation and even to slavery days. Nick LaRocca, son of the founder of the Original Dixieland Jazz band and the grandson of a local bandsman, plays the trumpet locally. Next to playing well, the best recommendation a young jazzman, black or white, can have is good family connections in the field of music, amply quartered and with banjos rampant. Recognizing this, the best locally-produced book on jazz is entitled *New Orleans Jazz: A Family Album.*

In America, conversations about families often turn into snobbish talk of the founding fathers. New Orleans has plenty of "old families." Suffice it to say that in the mid-1980's, the city is represented in the U.S. Congress by Corinne "Lindy" Claiborne Boggs, a lineal descendant of the first American governor of the Louisiana Territory, and Robert Livingston, a descendant of the brother of the man who nego-tiated the purchase of Louisiana from Napoleon.

No one has a monopoly on family pride. Walk into Jules Edwards' shoe repair shop at 3704 Magazine Street and you are confronted with a solid wall of photo-graphs of Mr. Edwards' forebears. Just above the counter where the proprietor re-ceives lost soles is a fine old portrait of Mr. Jules Dickerson, alias Dixon, a handsome light-skinned Negro from St. James Parish and Mr. Edwards' maternal grandfather, sitting proudly in the Civil War uniform of Company B of the United States Colored Volunteer Infantry. Next to Dickerson-Dixon is Edwards' paternal grandfather, the Reverend Edward Edwards of Moonshine, Louisiana, the Bible on one knee and a fancy tall hat on the other.

As everyone knows, illustrious families do not always produce illustrious off-spring. In fluid societies the black sheep discreetly disappear from sight, usually by moving away. In New Orleans they hang around. As a result, family talk in the Crescent City is surprisingly democratic. The aristocratic lady who appears at the Cadillac showroom to buy a $20,000 behemoth is as likely as not to discover that the double-knit salesman is actually kin to her.

This does not necessarily produce the best choice in cars, the most sound bank loans, or the wisest stock purchases, but it is undeniably cozy.

MONEY

*In which the lucre of New Orleanians
is examined and found to have
magnetic qualities but a low
specific gravity.*

Time is money

MONEY

New Orleans today has money, big money, nine-digit fortunes of the sort one expects to meet in Abu-Dabi, Muscat, or Bahrain.

One need only to attend the federal government's periodic auction of offshore oil fields to see those mountains of loot in the making. The mood is tense as tight-lipped men in well-tailored suits and lizard-skin boots gamble for high corporate stakes. It is not uncommon for oilmen to reap four or five dollars for every dollar bid successfully for tracts in the Gulf of Mexico—not a bad percentage.

To some, the money came easily. Grandpa owned some swamp land in Plaquemines Parish which he leased to trappers for the price of a few muskrat pelts. Then oil was discovered on it. Or, to take another case, Uncle Ernest, who spoke French, worked as a streetcar conductor in New Orleans. Then some California promoters hired him to interpret when they went out to buy up oil rights from Cajun farmers near Thibodaux. When he realized how easy it was, Ernest struck out for himself and now he has one hundred million dollars.

What effect does all this lucre have? Its impact is huge, of course, for money not only talks but can be quite loquacious. Yet in New Orleans there is another side to the old story. The impact of money there is moderated by the fact that New Orleans, unlike Houston or Dallas, was a major city even before the oil boom hit; its social hierarchies were already solidly in place. As a consequence, the macho new world of oil wealth has not been able to take over the town completely. This situation has brought frustration to some. Imagine the misfortune of striking it rich in the Tuscaloosa Trend, only to discover that a daily income of $10,000 does not unlock every door in the Crescent City. Worse, imagine the shock of discovering that you are being held at bay by an Establishment, more than a few members of which are of quite modest means—"Polish princesses," as oil-rich scoffers call them. To the oil-man, all this is disturbingly un-American.

But such is life in New Orleans. It remains one of the few American cities where the possession (or nonpossession) of wealth is not automatically considered evidence of a person's character. Membership in some of the best clubs costs little more than a dollar a day. Many who claim an income of well under six figures participate in all the local rites of what used to be called "society." It's a bargain.

How long this situation continues to prevail will depend on how much "new money" flows into the city. For in New Orleans and elsewhere, there is a kind of Gresham's Law which holds that new money eventually drives out old. This can bring great benefits to a community, for example, through an infusion of new ideas and fresh attitudes. But in the short run, at least, it also makes money more important. For whenever the tectonic plates of urban society start shifting, attention always focuses on the force that impels them, which is usually hard, cold cash.

CARPETBAGGERS AND COLONIALS

Port cities are rowdy and unmanageable places. They are also lucrative, and hence coveted. They are natural targets for takeovers. Where, for example, is the "free city" of Danzig today? Or Shanghai? Just look what's happening to Hong Kong.

As a port city, New Orleans is half golden goose and half sitting duck. It has been conquered three times already, once by the Spanish, once by the Americans, and once by the Union Army. A fourth *coup* is underway at the moment, this one led by multinational corporations.

New Orleanians are not faddists, but in the 1960's they went head over heels for the fashion of selling the family business. For a time it looked like selling out might replace work as a means of livelihood. And for a few, it actually did.

It is not easy to tell who is owned by whom in New Orleans. You must ferret out the information for yourself, often by reading the fine print on a firm's letterhead. In this way you can discover that the old soup factory down by the Industrial Canal is a wholly-owned subsidiary of some French manufacturer of buses. The same story is revealed by New Orleans' new skyscrapers. Most of them were built either by or for the big oil companies, usually to house their local satraps. The bosses sit in Houston and New York, and that's where the real decisions are made. With only two Fortune Five Hundred firms calling New Orleans home, it can be said that the Crescent City has become a colonial dependency, a domestic outpost of the Third World. This is not to say that local folks do not profit from this system. They do, to the point that the city could no longer survive without the multinationals. That's why the fourth *coup* has been a peaceful one, and why the conquerors are welcomed in many quarters.

Sometimes, though, a local firm stands up and fights. The imperial army of Colonel Sanders' Kentuckians and the Burger Kings of Miami were eyeing New Orleans covetously, when along came Popeye's, with its super-spicy fried chicken and steamy rice. All fast-food, mind you, served strictly stand-up at edifices of glass and formica. Popeye's took to the field—rolled back the alien attack, and is now carrying the battle into enemy territory. Having triumphed locally, Popeye's is colonizing the North. It is as if General Lee had reached Philadelphia and begun marching his troops on New York.

The fourth *coup* is carrying many new people to New Orleans in its wake. Some come to exploit the city as a market, while others seek to market New Orleans itself. Even the Jazz and Heritage Festival is a franchise operation run by the capable George Wein from his nerve center on Manhattan's Upper West Side. New Orleanians, it seems, make bad hucksters.

"Carpetbaggers" is not a nice word. But what if the carpetbagger's metabolism slows to the point that he does not take the money and run? Suppose he actually settles down in New Orleans? Suppose the Mobile Oil Co. vice-president refuses his transfer to L.A. so that he can keep on scrambling eggs from New Orleans' golden goose (with *grillades* and green Evangeline hot sauce, of course)?

Each year New Orleans' Metropolitan Area Committee assembles a conference for young leaders of the city. A major benchmark was recently reached by this conference when over half of its participants turned out to be "foreign" born. The acrid smell of burning carpetbags is in the air.

BOOSTERISM

Until recently, no list of the public attitudes of New Orleanians would have included boosterism. Quite the contrary. What little public bragging that occurred in the Crescent City ran to negatives: the worst weather; the most crime; the most corruption; the worst drivers; and so forth.

Now an entirely different mood has set in. Particularly among the young and upwardly mobile, boosterism is in fashion: New Orleans is on the move; New Orleans is aggressive, progressive; New Orleans will even surpass Atlanta, Dallas, Houston. Remember Sinclair Lewis's Babbitt, pounding on the big bass drum as he led the parade touting his home town of Zenith? Babbitt has now moved South, and New Orleans is the Zenith of the Sun Belt.

It is easy to ridicule this new boosterism, especially since many of its leading exponents are precisely those who are most likely to reap financial benefit from it. Skeptics would treat it more kindly, no doubt, if it brought benefits to more of those on the outs as well.

It is easy to criticize the new boosterism, too, as being somehow inappropriate to the ethos of the Crescent City. But those who make this particular claim take too short a view of things. They forget that the "new" banner waving is not new at all, that it flourished during the flush decades before the Civil War, when the city experienced its best days. The old homes and warehouses being so lovingly preserved today are monuments to the boosters and hucksters of the past. Like it or not, the men who founded family dynasties back in the 1820's would feel more at home among the new Babbitts of today than among many of their own descendants.

The pendulum will no doubt keep swinging back and forth between boosterism and *Schadenfreude,* the Germans' untranslatable word for the taking of pleasure in the misfortune of others. New Orleans will continue to be the greatest and the worst, depending on the fortunes of whoever is doing the evaluating. And just as surely, most people will continue to disbelieve the exaggerated claims on both sides.

Which would be a great misfortune. For New Orleans beyond all doubt possesses the most handsome neighborhoods, the nicest people, the sweetest citrus fruits, the best joke tellers, and the most beautiful women in the country, if not the world..

T R A N S P L A N T S

New Orleans is an aromatic city. It defines its smells and it is in turn defined by them. The reason is simple. Dense humidity and high temperatures pick up the slightest scent and hold it motionless in the air. Except when temporarily suppressed by rain, disturbed by air-conditioners, or sucked in by a million noses and as many automobile carburetors, the smells hang on until a change of seasons.

The olfactory calendar for summer is dominated by the pungent stench of rotting shellfish and garbage. But the months of October through March belong to the tiny white blossoms of the tea olive *(Osmanthus fragrans)*, also called the "sweet olive" or the "Italian olive." More than one casual visitor has ended up rearranging his whole life for the sake of this bewitching scent. An old local parfumerie, Hové, bottles a version of it to enable local ladies to preserve their microhabitat during trips to the North.

Recently, a New Orleans house guest was heard to rhapsodize over the ubiquitous tea olive as the very essence of New Orleans. An elderly native brought her up short by informing her, with studied patience, that "you know, of course, it is *not from here."*

Not from here? Indeed, the tea olive is not native to Louisiana. It was well established in New Orleans by 1800, however, which is a long time ago by most standards. Other seemingly native plants are "not from here" as well. They include okra, oleander *(Nerium oleander)*, camellia *(Camelia sasanqua)*, crape myrtle *(Lagerstroemis indica)*, and cape jasmine *(Gardenia jasminoides)*, not to mention lemons, oranges, figs, and pomegranates. All are imports, but all were quite at home on the Mississippi by 1800.

How fast does the American melting pot boil? The pace is nowhere the same. In raw-boned Phoenix, last year's arrival is an old-timer in comparison with this year's newcomer. In a few months, this season's new arrivals will seem well-rooted in comparison with those coming in the next wave.

Things move more slowly in New Orleans. Outsiders do become insiders, but the pace is definitely *adagio sostenuto.* Decades, even generations, can pass before the newcomer is fully accepted as part of the scene.

Incidentally, the brief interval between the tea olive month and the rotting garbage month is dominated by the sweetest, heaviest, and the most seductive scent of the year, that of Confederate Jasmine *(Trachelospermum jasminoides).* For several weeks the explosions of white blossoms take over the city, but they have not always done so. In the 1850's they, too, were transplanted here.

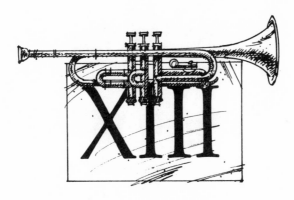

GENIUS

*In which New Orleanians
exhibit formidable talents
for some things
but not for others.*

Where no man has gone before

GENIUS

New Orleans can take anything in its stride, including genius. Or perhaps *especially* genius. A new chef or tight end for the Saints can become a local hero. Television interviewers will solicit their views on everything from childbearing to nuclear arms reduction. Ad agencies, nineteen columns of them in the *Yellow Pages*, can be enlisted to "hype" a rock star or touring bellydancer. But let a certified, card-carrying genius appear within Orleans Parish and he or she will be ignored.

John James Audubon reacted bitterly to such neglect by New Orleanians back in 1821. "I really believe now that my talents must be poor or else the country is," he wrote. Newcomers are often indignant about the Crescent City's reluctance to pay homage even to homegrown talent. "Why, in New York there'd be a statue...to x, or y, or z," they sputter.

And so there would. But in Manhattan the marble genius would quickly become isolated on his pedestal. Talk shows, Dior suits and chic parties would envelop him. Encapsulated by a cocoon of notoriety, the sources of his or her genius would soon run dry.

And so this paradox: New Orleans, by withholding from talent the corrupting influence of adulation, is a peculiarly hospitable environment in which to nurture talent, especially over the long term. Surrealist photographer Clarence John Laughlin may be feted in Paris, but on Marigny Street he was still, at age 79, "funny old Clarence."

Incidentally, Beethoven's sublimely beautiful Opus 59 quartets were produced when the composer was giving piano lessons around Vienna and playing second violin in Prince Razumovosky's amateur quartet. Vienna is another city that takes genius in stride.

UNEMPLOYMENT

The greatest mind ever produced within the boundaries of Orleans Parish, Louisiana, ended his days as an unemployed and mentally unstable fop. He took breakfast every day in the building on Royal Street that now houses Brennan's.

Since it was also his home, he did not need an expense account to dine there. After breakfast he would place monocle to eye, take his walking stick in hand, and stroll towards Canal Street. Promenading up and down, he ogled the ladies and doffed his hat courteously to friends, both real and imaginary.

Paul Morphy was a lawyer, which has absolutely nothing to do with his intellectual eminence. His colleagues at the bar, however, can thank their lucky stars that he never practiced, for he started out by memorizing the entire *Code Civil.* Then he lost interest in it—not enough of a challenge, one may suppose. Such antics, along with those imaginary friends and his even more numerous imaginary enemies, caused people to worry about Morphy's sanity. Long after Paul Morphy's death, one of Sigmund Freud's greatest disciples, Ernest Jones, wrote a whole book psychoanalyzing the poor man.

The one thing that Morphy stuck with was chess, but even that did not hold his attention for long. No all-American boy, the young Morphy hated sports. He preferred the ancient drawing room game that was all the rage in Paris in the 1840's, and hence in Creole New Orleans as well. By age thirteen he had beaten his father and every other chess player in town.

With no further action locally, he had to choose between retiring to junior high or seeking new frontiers. He took up chess full time. At the age of twenty Morphy issued a challenge "to every chess player in New York," not to mention the entire membership of the New York Chess Club, whom he proposed to take on simultaneously in as many separate games as necessary. He obliterated everyone who came forward to play. Then he went on to London and Paris and knocked out all comers there, including the reigning masters of the day. His specialty in Europe was to take on a half dozen of the best players at once, blindfolded.

Oliver Wendell Holmes hailed young Morphy's achievement as a "triumph of the American intellect." And so it was. But Morphy's methods were so lacking in Yankee brashness and impetuosity as to make him seem positively un-American. The usual way to open a chess match back then was the Evans gambit, a fast attack move in the spirit of the Boston Celtics or the Dallas Cowboys. This was not for Morphy. He generally chose to hang back. With true Creole cunning, he would quietly maneuver his men into place, being sure to keep his queen safely out of the way of harassment. Then, just as his opponent was preening himself on his own strong opening, Morphy would spring the trap. Whoosh!

New Orleans' contribution to the most cerebral of games represents the triumph of the stiletto over the bludgeon, the schemer and strategist over the showy tactician. But once Morphy had vanquished everyone on earth in his field, what more was there for him to do? Practice law? Sell insurance? The man did have problems.

162

MEMORY

When Mr. Daniel Moriarty's wife died back in the 1880's, he built an enormous tomb for her in New Orleans' Metairie Cemetery. The massive obelisk, clearly visible today from Interstate 10, is flanked by four draped female figures. Local wags claim they represent Faith, Hope, Charity—and Mrs. Moriarty. But the fourth figure is actually that of Memory.

A fitting monument for the city as a whole. For in New Orleans, creativity arises less from fantasizing about the future than from mental wanderings through the past. Second and third generation Italians, nostalgic for an Italy that never was, produced the zany and imaginative Piazza d'Italia. Compare this with the work of future-looking developers, whose bland image of the coming age imposes yet more forgettable "modern" architecture on the city each year.

Which leads to the strange case of Louis Moreau Gottschalk. Born on Rampart Street, Gottschalk was a musical prodigy by the age of five, America's first piano virtuoso by age ten, and her greatest composer of the nineteenth century by age twenty-five. Chopin and Berlioz judged him to be a genius.

Because his mother dragged him off to France in his twelfth year, it is said that Gottschalk was a New Orleanian only by virtue of his birth certificate. But this is not quite the case. The early compositions that won him the greatest acclaim are all built on musical themes connected with daily life in his native city. True, those compositions were written in France, but under most extraordinary circumstances.

It was the spring of 1848 and the French capital was shaken by revolutionary upheavals. The nineteen-year-old Gottschalk wisely accepted an invitation from a friend to flee to the quiet of Clermont-de-l'Oise, a village forty miles from Paris. The same friend generously arranged a small house for him to live in, and suggested that he might wish to take meals with the learned and cultured doctors connected with a small mental asylum there. He did.

Some years earlier, Gottschalk had been stricken with fever, the legacy of his boyhood in malaria-ridden New Orleans. During a pause in his delirium he had scrawled down some melodies that had been swirling in his mind. Later he filed the sheet of musical shorthand with the rest of his papers. One day at lunch with the medical doctors, the conversation turned to the question of what people are capable of accomplishing while in an unconscious state. A doctor asserted that great creative acts could occur under just such conditions.

Gottschalk perked up. He recalled the musical notes he had penned during his bout of fever. Reexamining them now, he discovered that they contained melodies recollected from his earliest boyhood on Rampart Street in New Orleans: street

163

songs, Caribbean melodies and slave chants from what was then called Congo Square, just down the block from his family's home on Rampart Street. He immediately elaborated them into full compositions and arranged them for solo piano. That autumn he performed them in Paris. Gottschalk's world renown as a composer dates from than moment.

Listening to Gottschalk's *Bamboula, Le Bananier,* or *The Banjo,* are you startled that they anticipate ragtime music and even early jazz by half a century? Yet it is no less startling that these trail-blazing works of American music sprang from Gottschalk's deepest unconscious memory, that they looked backward rather than forward in time.

A near contemporary of Gottschalk's, the black Creole poet Armand Lanusse, shared Gottschalk's state of mind, and wrote in 1836:

> *La Passé! La Passé! C'est là qu'est mon étoile*
> *C'est là qu'est mon trésor.*
> (The past! The past! There is my star,
> and There is my treasure.)

Camille Thierry, another black Creole poet from New Orleans, put the same thought even more succinctly:

> *J'aime a me souvenir.*
> (I love to reminisce.)

EXPLORERS

New Orleans has been home to two great explorers, Sir Henry Morton Stanley and Mr. Martin Green. Stanley, the illegitimate child of Welsh parents, escaped from the workhouse and made his way to New Orleans as a cabin boy. A Crescent City merchant adopted him and gave him his own name. After discovering the elusive Dr. Livingstone near Lake Tanganyika in 1871, Stanley went on to explore the Congo River and some of the most exotic real estate in Central Africa.

Unlike Stanley, Martin Green is not about to leave the New Orleans area even long enough to be knighted. His home is on Lapeyrousse Street in the Seventh Ward. Part Negro, part French and part East Indian, he has always been busy. He served briefly in France during World War II and is at this moment visiting a lady friend over in Opelousas. "At my age you can't afford to miss a chance," he wryly observes.

Martin Green stays close to his native city, but with the help of his imagination he roams the outer limits of space. A high school drop-out, Green has visited strange galaxies and exotic planets unknown to NASA, and with paint and brush he has recorded everything he has seen.

Scores of large canvases and half a dozen huge murals reveal the breadth of Green's visionary explorations. He presents a realm of fiery suns, ice-blue skies, and enormous volcanoes spewing orange flames into the black night. The scenes are on a scale that dwarfs Albert Bierstadt's romantic images of the Rockies. But Martin Green's style is definitely primitive—black light poster paint, broad brush strokes, etc. He is the Grandma Moses of outer space.

Green pursues his fantasies with a passion. He has covered the walls of his own home with paintings, and is readying scaffolding to do the ceiling as soon as he can come to an understanding with his landlord. Michelangelo never had such problems.

Even if the ceiling does not get painted, this wiry and energetic man from Lapeyrousse Street is the best traveled person in the Seventh Ward.

PATRONAGE

Recently the National Endowment for the Arts came to New Orleans. It seems that some advisory committee had instructed the agency to "do something for Jazz, our uniquely American art form."

To receive the benefits of this solicitude, some five dozen local musicians were summoned to an audience with The Endowment. Among them were a few who had been playing jazz since the music was in its cradle. Together, they represented nearly a millennium of experience in jazz. The musicians looked scruffy. The Endowment was outfitted by Anne Klein.

"You must learn to write a good application," The Endowment exclaimed, sitting on a tall director's stool. "And our peer review committees pay special attention to support letters." (Grammatical note: in The Endowment, nouns modify nouns.)

About this time, a young black player stood up to ask if he could get money for Latin jazz. Not a bad question, in fact, since Jelly Roll Morton himself had insisted that all true jazz has a dash of Latin spice in it.

But no, this was not to be. The director's chair informed him that The Endowment does not support Latin jazz.

Now an old-timer took the floor. To understand what happened, the reader should recall that *St. Louis Blues* consists of three strains, the middle one ("St. Louis woman, with all your diamond rings...") being decidedly a Latin tango.

"Suppose," he said, "that I was W.C. Handy and I wanted one of them grants to write *St. Louis Blues...*"

The musicians were all paying attention now.

"You're telling me," he continued, "that you folks would give out money for the first and third strains of *St. Louis Blues,* but you won't pay me to write the second, right?"

The response was drowned in hoots and laughter.

PATERNITY

"King Bolden and myself were the first men that began
playing Jazz in the city of dear old New Orleans. . . "
—Willie G. "Bunk" Johnson

"Here Lies the World's First Man in Jazz."
—Inscription on the tomb of Nick LaRocca, New Orleans

"The Originator of Jazz."
—Inscription of tomb of Emile "Stalebread" Lacoume, New Orleans

"I invented Jazz."
—Ferdinand "Jelly Roll" Morton

ECCENTRICS

In the sweepstakes for bizarre characters, New Orleans is in the big leagues—world class, in fact. Its only near competitors are Shanghai in the old days, Istanbul before Ataturk cleaned things up, and Marseilles when the Sixth Fleet is in.

It has always been this way. William Faulkner's life in Oxford, Mississippi, had not prepared him for the eccentricity he encountered when he moved to the Crescent City. Faulkner began his literary apprenticeship in the mid-twenties as a contributor to the *Times-Picayune* and *Double Dealer*, filling story after story with descriptions of the city's longshoremen, gamblers, cops, and winos. Benjy Compson, the idiot-hero of the novel, *The Sound and the Fury,* is modeled directly on a prototype Faulkner observed in the French Quarter.

The parade of eccentrics marches on today. The half-witted but lovable "Ruthie the Duck Lady" still makes her daily rounds on Royal Street, although she is temporarily without a duck to lead about on a string. The middle-aged man who reads Homer's *Iliad* in the original Greek while sitting with a six-pack of Dixie Beer each afternoon in Lafayette Park is still plugging away, or was, until they took the benches away.

The only difference from Faulkner's time is that eccentricity is now becoming professionalized. Its practitioners expect to be remunerated for doing just as they like, as if this required special effort on their part. You can't buy a tin cup in town.

Fortunately, behind the highly visible professional eccentrics there remains a whole battalion of crypto-eccentrics in New Orleans, each of them chasing his own will-o'-the-wisp without the slightest regard for the opinion of society. One of the best local lawyers possesses the world's premier collection of mid-nineteenth-century Parisian douche machines. An insurance man paints his house violet, inside and out, while an otherwise elegant and refined lady loves nothing better than to scream and howl at the Monday night wrestling matches in the down-river suburb of St. Bernard.

Such people are to human society as the spices are to gumbo, or those occasional splashes of bright color are to a subdued portrait by Degas. Without them, blandness would reign supreme. What city in America can claim so many spices in its kitchen, so many colors on its palette, as New Orleans?

The line between someone who is eccentric and someone who is just plain crazy is thin, especially in New Orleans. In the Crescent City, the adjective "crazy" is actually a kind of compliment, indicating independence of mind, contempt for mere conformity, and a healthy readiness to *épaté la bourgeoisie.* Of course, extravagant impracticality can be taken to extremes, and with tragic results. Suicide is not uncommon in New Orleans. As early as 1875 the *Picayune* reported on New Orleanians' mania for self destruction. To be sure, this ultimate form of eccentricity is illegal in Louisiana, as it is elsewhere. But illegal or not, suicide in New Orleans has its own etiquette, according to which members of society are expected to leap from the Mississippi River Bridge and others from the Huey Long.

SCIENCE

*In which
perplexing instances are invoked
to show that what really exists
can be more intriguing than
what seems to exist.*

A basic lesson in tension/compression

SCIENCE

What do Kitty Carlyle, Mel Ott, Truman Capote, Lillian Hellman, Antoine "Fats" Domino, and Dorothy Lamour have in common? They were all born in New Orleans.

So were E.H. Sothern, the finest Shakespearean actor of the nineteenth century; George Herriman, the illustrator of *Archie and Mahitabel;* Victor Sejour, the black Creole poet; and Ernest Gireaud, who gained membership in the *Academie français* for his orchestrations of Bizet's *Carmen* and Offenbach's raucous *Gaiete parisien.*

A city is a school that provides cradle-to-grave education for all its citizens, twenty-four hours a day. But not all cities offer the same curriculum. Leipzig in Germany somehow turns out scientists like pancakes. Edinburgh has produced more than its share of philosophers; Vienna has always spawned musicians, while tiny Williamsburg, Virginia, specialized in statesmen during its brief flowering.

Where, then, do New Orleans' special gifts lie? Obviously in music of all types, and also in acting and in the writing of colorful prose. But not yet in science. Only one member of the National Academy of Sciences resides in the city, and he hails from Warsaw (the one in Poland, not Warsaw, Louisiana). New Orleans natives are also conspicuous by their rarity among the membership of the National Academy of Medicine, the National Institute of Engineering, and the ranks of Nobel Prize laureates in science.

It is true that New Orleanians have spearheaded impressive work in various areas of applied science, notably in public health and meteorology—two fields that affect everyone—and that local medicine can claim some genuine innovators, such as Dr. Rudolph Matas, who helped advance vascular surgery half a century ago. But these are exceptions. The Crescent City's deepest affection has been withheld from science and high technology.

Why so few scientists? Perhaps because science is possible only when events can be made to repeat themselves, or at least can be checked. This is scarcely the situation in whimsical and capricious New Orleans.

The French philosopher René Descartes declared that: "All my life I delighted in the use of reason more than memory...." New Orleans is precisely the opposite, a more subjective place, a city that lives on reminiscences and feeling rather than on the cool and objective analysis of reality. In the American brain, New Orleans represents the right hemisphere, not the left.

But not completely, for the passion for hard knowledge is universal. Even in 1903 there were New Orleanians who saw themselves standing in the great tradition of Bacon, Newton, and Darwin. Among them was the editor of *The Times Picayune,*

173

who introduced his paper's definitive (yes, definitive) Creole cookbook by referring to New Orleans as a place "where the art of good cooking was long ago reduced to a positive science."

ENGINEERING

Since the Industrial Revolution, a new form of urban bravado has entered the scene: engineering. London's Crystal Palace and the Eiffel Tower in Paris put their respective cities on the technological map. It remained for delirious New York to make a cult of engineering, beginning with the Roebling Brothers' Brooklyn Bridge and reaching full flower in today's hundred-story glass skyscrapers. New York set the pace, and as Manhattan goes, so goes the nation.

It was only recently that New Orleans opened its first shrines to the Goddess of Engineering. The Greater New Orleans Mississippi River Bridge is one of the nation's larger spans and enables the curious to find out what Algiers and Gretna look like from the air. The levees and hydraulic system would be impressive if they were more visible, but they are not. Some of the fanciest engineering in town is to be seen in the port facilities stretching thirty miles along the river. But thanks to the levees, they too are out of sight.

So what can one show Uncle Ralph, the structural engineer from Portland, when he comes to town for the Shriners' convention? Assuming that he has any interest other than to discover whether Storyville has been reopened, take him around to see *Quercus virginianae*. Let him gaze at this marvel of engineering. Preen yourself as he acknowledges—correctly—that neither San Francisco nor Chicago has anything like it. Swell with pride as he calculates the mighty stresses held at bay by the graceful structure. Offer to take his photograph in front of this marvel.

Quercus virginianae of the family *Fagaceae* is better known as the live oak. It thrives all over the Deep South, but it has nowhere been urbanized more successfully than in New Orleans. Standing twelve to fourteen meters high, it may spread sideways to double its height or better. And this is where the engineering comes in.

Take one of those live oak branches reaching across St. Charles Avenue. Its entire mass of several score tons is suspended from one point where the branch joins the trunk. To appreciate this triumph of engineering, try holding a desk chair at arm's length. It's not easy. If you are mathematically inclined, you can calculate the stress on your shoulder, or on the oak's trunk, quite easily. First, you must locate the "centroid," which is the point of balance if the branch alone were to be suspended freely. Multiply the distance from the centroid to the trunk by the weight of the entire branch. The resulting figure is the "moment." Then divide the weight of the entire branch by the cross-sectional area of the branch at its junction with the trunk. That produces what is called the "shear stress." Add the "shear stress" to the "moment" and you have the total stress born by the trunk for that one branch. Then do the same for all the other branches. Finally, carry out the same calculations for the roots which stretch out horizontally from the trunk underground.

The resulting figure represents the total stress carried by one *Quercus virginianae*. Multiply this by the number of live oaks on New Orleans' major streets and boulevards and you have a staggering figure, quite enough to dazzle your Uncle Ralph.

Apparently, what Walt Whitman called the "rude, unbending, lusty" quality of New Orleans' live oaks also bothers some people—even threatens them. Why else would the Federal Highway Administration, with the approval of the local Chamber of Commerce, have gone out of their way to destroy one of the finest avenues of *Querci virginianae* in the world by driving Interstate 10 down the middle of Claiborne Avenue?

WISDOM

The man who, in the words of his biographer, "liberated the South from its preoccupation with race," is a New Orleanian. Not just any New Orleanian, mind you, but one who weighed in at less than one hundred pounds when he entered college and still went out for football. At eighty, he still walks with a cane but remains vigorous, brisk of gesture. Judge John Minor Wisdom is just the man to have explained what the Supreme Court meant when it said that segregation should be dismantled "with all deliberate speed."

Wisdom belongs to that gracious and quixotic breed of humanity that long inhabited New Orleans' Uptown District. A veteran of Miss Lewis' dancing classes (class of 1920), Wisdom knows how to have a good time. He also knows when to be serious. Like many New Orleanians, he despised Huey Long's tin-horn tyranny.

Unlike most of his neighbors, John Wisdom went all out in his opposition to the demagogic Democrat, even to the point of joining what was then an almost nonexistent Republican Party of Louisiana. Decades later his new party took the governorship.

An historian's historian, Wisdom is steeped in the past of his beloved state. From his years of private study he culled material for his brilliantly argued opinion in *U.S. vs. Louisiana*, which destroyed the legal basis for racial discrimination in voting rights. His argument is virtually a history of the state's law on the subject.

In opinion after opinion, Wisdom and his three colleagues on the Fifth Circuit Court of Appeals struck down segregation in the South. They attacked it in the schools, the universities, in public facilities, and in the voting booth.

It is easy to make revolutions against strangers, which is why most revolutionaries put as much distance—psychological as well as physical—between themselves and their opponents. John Minor Wisdom was formed by the world he changed. He is part of it, and he cares about it—which made his task infinitely more delicate, his victories the more enduring, and his opponents the more respectful of him.

LOST WISDOM

Coupé zoré milet fait pas chouval.
(Cutting off a mule's ear won't make him a horse.)

Parole trop fort, machoir gonfle.
(Loud talk swells the jaw.)

Capon vives longtemps.
(The coward lives a long time.)

Chien pas mangé chien.
(Dogs don't eat dogs.)

Di moin qui vous laimien, ma di vous qui vous yé.
(Tell me whom you love, and I'll tell you who you are.)

Merci pas couté arien.
(Thanks costs nothing.)

INTELLIGENCE

New Orleans is a center of advanced intelligence, not of the kind that scores high on college board tests, but of that peculiar breed that ferrets out international intrigue. Of this, the Crescent City has more than its share.

To discover the reasons, one need look no further than the port, now the country's largest in terms of tonnage. Stretching for miles along the Mississippi, it is virtually impossible to patrol. It is a perfect place to jump ship, as thousands have done, or to bring in drugs—although the wild coastal marshes are even better for this.

New Orleans thus provides a salubrious environment for spying. A Bulgarian "sailor" with a forty-eight hour shore leave can taxi to the airport, catch a plane to Denver to pick up a package, return to New Orleans, and still have time for dinner at K-Paul's before U.S. Immigration starts looking for him. This actually happens.

Because of all this activity, the FBI maintains a hundred-man office (Tel. 504-522-4671) in The Big Easy. The agents could tell some rousing tales of organized crime, Libyan hitmen, anti-regime Polish seamen trying to jump ship and being forced back on board, and hanky-panky involving Soviet cruise ships.

In order to limit the sphere in which intelligence is gathered (and also to retaliate agianst Soviet curbs on the American diplomats in Russia), the FBI has designated certain areas of South Lousiana off-limits to all people whose names end in "ich," "ov," or "ski," and also to anyone professing too keen a love for brown bread and caviar. Soviet citizens cannot set foot in Moisant Field, for example, nor can they drive down the I-10 highway. This wise policy limits the Kremlin's access to such critical facilities as Denny's Restaurant at Williams Boulevard, The King's Harem Massage Parlor in Fat City, and the Snake Farm in LaPlace.

FBI agents view New Orleans as a good post. Bud Mullen rose from Special-Agent-in-Charge in New Orleans to become Assistant Director of the FBI, and then head of drug enforcement nationally. A former number two in New Orleans was promoted to direct the FBI's Washington operations.

The FBI's work is not all cloak-and-dagger, however. Some visiting Soviet diplomats rented a car while in town and promptly got lost in the city's non-Euclidean geometry. Their American "tail" sympathized. Pulling them over, he gave them directions. They graciously acknowledged the help with a Muscovite "Tenkyeu!"

SUBVERSION

In the year 1976, the Soviet Union, after two decades of trying, finally achieved military parity with the United States in certain key areas. Détente still held, but the superpower confrontation was heating up daily behind the scenes in Washington, Moscow—and New Orleans. The stakes were high: The Future of Civilization As We Know It.

It was in that year of 1976 that representatives of the Union of Soviet Socialist Republics approached Mr. Blaine Kern, builder of many of the grand floats for Mardi Gras parades. Casablanca was closed, so the KGB's emissary chose the next best spot for the rendezvous—Algiers, just across the Mississippi from Jackson Square, and the site of Kern's atelier. The proposal was fantastic: You use our good Russian tractors to pull every float in Mardi Gras, and the Kremlin will make them available to you practically for nothing. Kern would become rich and the *Vladimirets* tractor (literally, the "Vladimirian," i.e., from Vladimir Lenin) would become as American as apple pie or Datsun.

Blaine Kern is a practical man. He saw the benefits lurking in the offer. He liked the low price tag on the "Vladimirian," and he liked the fact that the machines would be serviced by a good ol' boy from nearby Mississippi who had no resemblance whatsoever to the KGB heavies in James Bond movies. And so Kern bought a few.

Then the sky fell. Irate letters to the local press and indignant phone calls indicated that Kern had threatened the Republic and imperiled The Future of Civilization As We Know It, in Algiers and elsewhere throughout the East and West Banks.

And so Blaine Kern drew back, albeit not completely. Which is why some, but not many of the tractors in Mardi Gras, come from the *Belarus* factory in Minsk.

POLITICS

*In which a means to an end
turns out to be an end in itself,
in spite of what our founding fathers
may have wished.*

Prime only: When the elite, they all meet

182

POLITICS

Mayor Ernest "Dutch" Morial once said that "Our major local product in New Orleans is politics." The Chamber of Commerce may disagree, but Dutch was right. Every other product of the Crescent City is turned out during the forty-hour week. But politics is produced round the clock on triple shifts with no vacations. Unlike manufacturing, the industry of politics embraces the entire population. Where else will three-quarters of all registered voters turn out for a primary? With the sole exceptions of food and Carnival, politics has no close rival for the attention of New Orleanians.

In New Orleans, *everything* is political. Museums are political, hospitals are political, births are political, deaths are political. Nobody considering residence there should switch his registration until he is confident he can decipher the political coefficient of any subject under the sun, from aardvarks to zymurgy.

Why such a passion for politics? Don't look to the political scientists for answers. Their usual argument is that New Orleans is a city in transition. They claim that the rapid changes in the local economy and in the social make-up of the parish are forcing great decisions on the public. Politics, they reason, is where those decisions are made and is therefore of interest to all.

But the world is full of cities in transition and most of them are politically apathetic. As to the Great Decisions thesis—rubbish! Far from helping politics, the need to reach Great Decisions only hurts politics, for it renders the enterprise all too serious. If you want a real political fight, make sure the stakes are as low as possible.

The one political analyst with something serious to say on the subject is Professor Gordon Saussy of the University of New Orleans. Saussy points out that New Orleans' charter calls for the election of far more local officials than in any other big city in America. The justice system alone requires elections to be held for all judges, for the District Attorney, for both a criminal and civil sheriff, for four clerks of court, two registrars, and two constables. The ballot looks like a menu at Galatoire's.

New Orleans, then, uses the ballot box to select countless officials who could just as easily be appointed. But even this is not the whole story, for this practice is as much an effect of politicization as it is a cause. The true cause, which has somehow escaped notice until this moment, is that the Crescent City lacks major professional sports. The Pelicans died ages ago and they never were in baseball's big leagues. Out-of-town entrepreneurs tried to foist a basketball team on the Crescent City, but quickly gave up and moved the franchise to Utah. In-town entrepreneurs tried to turn the same trick with their USFL franchise, the Breakers, but the made-for-TV football did not gain enough fire power and appeal in New Orleans. The Saints are now playing a respectable brand of pro football; but this keeps life stirred up for only a few months in the autumn. That leaves most of the year with no other major entertainment than Mardi Gras. Politics fills the breach.

Elders of the community will assure you that New Orleanians have always been addicted to politics. They recite the words of an English tourist, Thomas Ashe, who observed in 1806 that: "The Americans, since their arrival here, have been so occupied by politics...that their minds have never been sufficiently unbent to form a course of pleasures for themselves." Times have indeed changed. Now it is possible to practice politics and still have "a course of pleasure." This constitutes progress.

POWER STRUCTURE

Scarcely a year goes by in which at least one counterculture journalist does not produce an exposé on New Orleans' invisible power structure. Strange to say, though, the power structures thus exposed are never the same.

And with good reason: New Orleans has no power structure. At least, not in the sense of a neat pyramid ascending to some single lofty pinnacle. It would be much easier if it did. Decisions could be taken quickly, results measured, responsibility fixed.

Instead, New Orleans is a city of fiefdoms. A chart of its "power structure" would look like a Harvard Business School analysis of the Holy Roman Empire. Back in 1836, when the newly-arrived Americans became frustrated in their attempts to unseat the local Creole establishment, they pushed through a charter that split the city into three separate municipalities, virtually three separate cities. Each controlled its own finances, streets, police, etc. New Orleans was balkanized, divided up like Poland of old, but by the hands of its own citizens rather than by external enemies. This outlandish arrangement was revoked in 1852, but soon thereafter the urban pie was sliced anew into separate portions, and then still other ones, and still others yet.

Many continue today. Some slices correspond to political wards, others are cultural, racial, or religious. Each has its own power structure, with only the most fragile links binding them all together at the top. In a sense, the three old municipalities have even been revived in the division of greater New Orleans into the three parishes of Orleans, St. Bernard, and Jefferson.

To a Chicagoan, accustomed to the legacy of Mayor Daley's centralization, this can only appear as grossly inefficient. But it forces a lot of people to talk with one another who otherwise might not do so. It also encourages a degree of humility in New Orleanians, since no one can pretend to control everything.

Perhaps this is one of the reasons why as great a man as the poet Goethe could have regretted the passing of the Holy Roman Empire.

TAXES

Taxation without representation is tyranny, declared the American colonists. A splendid line, of course, but what does it really mean? Does it imply that taxation *with* representation is just fine? New Orleanians would consider such a conclusion to be the height of foolishness. They would finish the proclamation differently: that representation without taxation is the goal of all prudent governments—in a word, bliss.

Bliss has reigned in the Crescent City since time immemorial. Local tax levies are only a third of those in Boston or New York. The state income tax in Louisiana is about the lowest in the nation, except for Alabama. And property taxes, a queer invention of Anglo-Saxon Yankees, have yet to take firm hold in the Creole belt. In the early 1980's, fewer than one out of five New Orleans homeowners paid any property taxes at all.

The entire governmental system of New Orleans is a monument to the sacred principle that representation can and should prevent taxation. Long before anyone heard of Proposition 13, or California for that matter, New Orleans had been constituted in such a way as to obviate the need for tax repeals.

The first line of defense in keeping the government out of your pocket is to elect anti-tax local officials. When a mayoral candidate recently advanced the radical notion that someone earning $50,000 could afford to pay $222 in city income tax, he was rewarded with six percent of the vote. It is also important to elect anti-tax candidates to the state legislature. This has been accomplished with staggering effectiveness. In just one session of the Louisiana Legislature in 1982, the sum of $12 million in exemptions to the sales tax was awarded and the state itself was exempted from paying sales taxes. Together, such exemptions add up to billions.

The second line of defense is to be sure that the local tax assessors are all elected, thus assuring that these gentlemen will undo any mischief the mayor and city council may perpetrate.

Next to being an admiral in the Austrian navy, the position of tax assessor in New Orleans is one of the best sinecures around. Each district has one, and the posts are passed from father to son like duck hunting camps in the marshlands. The work is simple. If taxes are raised, they lower assessments accordingly. If an old widow loses her pension, the assessor will lower her assessment still more. The assessors are watchdogs of the private purse, and they are elected not to bite the hand that feeds them. Pity other American cities, where there is only one assessor and he is appointed by the mayor!

But what about all those community services that should be financed through taxes? Well, the potholes in the streets serve a useful function by forcing drivers to slow down. Transportation and education are more problematic, but tight budgets keep the bureaucrats from wasting the public's hard-earned money on frills. As to all the other things the money might be spent on, will they really raise the quality of life or just change it, and perhaps in ways one may not want?

The power to tax is the power to govern. No taxes, no government—at least not in the normal sense of the word. Political philosophers describe this state as anarchy, and some of the greatest radicals among them have tried to picture how such a society would work. If they would take a walk down the streets of New Orleans, they could find out.

COOPTATION

No political art has been honed to a finer edge in New Orleans than cooptation. With nearly three centuries of practice, the true New Orleanian can detect in a flash whom he can brush off, whom he must fight, and whom he has to coopt.

If cooptation is called for, the quarry must be stalked and an appropriate trap set. One person can be coopted by being brought in on a business deal, another might require membership in a club or on a board, still a third needs an option on some real estate. The actual catch takes place with a truly Einsteinian conservation of energy. Not one more ounce of bait is expended than is necessary to bag the game. Then snap! The trap is sprung, and the prey is rendered harmless. He becomes part of the system, coopted.

Every art is built up slowly, but every art also has its one sure genius, the fellow who sets the standard for all who follow. In fishing, for instance, the distinction goes to Izaak Walton, the genial author, in 1563, of *The Compleat Angler*. In cooptation the laurels go to New Orleans' turn-of-the-century mayor, Paul Capdeville.

The moustachioed Capdeville was elected to office at a time when crime raged unchecked throughout the city. No section was spared the effects of thievery, swindling, and murder. The criminal element seemed ubiquitous. Its headquarters and main base of operations was a hangout known unofficially as the Terminal Saloon on Basin Street, just off Canal. Among the Terminal gang one could find thugs and cutthroats ready to commit any act of villainy for a price.

Capdeville assessed the situation—stalked his prey. He could not ignore the gangsters, nor could he hope to beat them in a fight. So he chose cooptation. One fine day in 1904 he strode into the Terminal Saloon and, under the watchful eye of the proprietor, swore everyone present into the ranks of the New Orleans Police Department. Editorial writers were outraged, but the tactic succeeded. In a wink of an eye, it became more dangerous to be a criminal than a policeman.

If someone were ever to write a textbook on cooptation, he should devote a whole chapter to the importance of doing the job thoroughly. It's fine to conserve bait, but dangerous when your trophy starts looking hungry again. This, too, has been known to happen in New Orleans.

GRUDGES

Nothing is ever settled in New Orleans. Did you lose a vote at your club or board meeting? No bother. Just get to work and be patient. Bring the same proposal back later as if nothing happened. When it passes this time, be sure to smile at the folks who voted the measure down earlier. Or perhaps that used car you bought in Mississippi was assessed at too high a figure for the Louisiana registration tax? Don't blow up at the assessor. Just go back to City Hall during his lunch hour and try again with one of his colleagues. Once you achieve your end, be sure to nod graciously at the first guy as he returns from Café Maspero.

Notice carefully what happens to you as you engage in such shenanigans. Gradually, the settling of scores with that leader of the rival faction or with the tax assessor becomes more important than the specific issue before you. As that happens, you are well on your way to becoming a true New Orleanian. Throughout the Deep

South people live by the motto, "Don't get mad, just get even." A century of life as underdogs led many residents of the Crescent City to elevate this practice to an art. It is a demanding one, however. It takes patience, lots of time, and a long, long memory.

The history of New Orleans politics is the history of grudges, and so is the history of countless nonpolitical organizations and groups locally. Time and time again organizations arrive at decisions that are absolutely inexplicable in terms of the immediate interests of those involved. Only when you discover that the leader of faction "A" harbors a grudge against a member of faction "B" can you understand what is really happening. The grudge is what counts. The specific issue is merely the stage on which the grudge is acted out.

A well-tended grudge can last for years, even decades. This can turn daily life into a rather tricky mine field. Suppose, for example, that Arrington walks into a bar while you are having a drink with Pellittiere. You should be aware that Arrington's brother-in-law was responsible for all the problems Pellittiere's daddy had with the IRS back in the 1950's, which in turn forced Pellittiere to drop out of college. Twenty-six years later, the old grudge is still active. The fact that outward cordiality may reign at that bar will not prevent Pellittiere from associating you with the force that had thwarted his aspirations. Pellittiere has now built you into the structure of his grudge world, and with consequences that might someday amaze you.

Granted, there are a few New Orleanians who put the very notion of grudges out of their minds. They act as if grudges don't exist. Standing tall, they let their virtue radiate its warmth to all around them.

Far more numerous are those who acknowledge the ubiquity of grudges and endeavor to steer a safe course among them. To succeed at this, you must stay out of public life until you have programmed your mental floppy disk with data on a minimum of one hundred ancient animosities. Any fewer would be dangerous, for you could blunder into the middle of a festering grudge completely unawares, like someone who wanders into the crossfire of two armies that he thought were at peace.

This approach to the grudge problem is demanding, but it brings many rewards, aesthetic as well as practical. It is a first step toward connoisseurship in the matter of grudges. For grudges in New Orleans are like wine, to be savored and appreciated, albeit in small quantities. Like wines, some grudges peak early, while others acquire a deep, rich bouquet over the years. Like wine, too, every grudge in New Orleans eventually turns sour, which is reason enough to remain a teetotaler in this domain.

188

GAINES AND LOSSES

When some matter does get settled in New Orleans — and scarcely a year goes by without one or two such occurrences—it is invariably the product of sheer tenacity. It may be the tenacity someone shows in promoting his or her cause, or the greater tenacity of someone else in opposing it. But endurance counts.

If ever a noble monument is raised to doggedness, its alabaster pedestal should be surmounted with the figure of Myra Clark Gaines, a New Orleanian. The field on which she chose to demonstrate her mastery of the arts of perseverance was the court of law. She pressed her life-long case, *Gaines vs. New Orleans*, in thirty trials involving up to three hundred defendants at a time. She employed lawyers from Philadelphia, Baltimore, and New Orleans to toil on her behalf, and toil they did. They carried *Gaines vs. New Orleans* to the Louisiana Supreme Court five times and to the United States Supreme Court no fewer than seventeen times.

It all began 1834. When the U.S. Supreme Court finished hearing the fifth appeal of the case is 1853, one justice, in obvious relief, wrote that

> When some distinguished American lawyer shall retire from practice to write a history of his country's jurisprudence, this case will be registered by him as one of the most remarkable in the records of the courts.

It was to be more remarkable than the justice suspected, for the case was still dragging on nearly four decades later. Myra Gaines herself was dead by then, but she had infected her old lawyer with her doggedness and he continued to sue for his fees.

What was at stake? For one thing, large sections of the city of New Orleans: whole faubourgs, including hundreds of homes, plantations, businesses, and rents and returns that grew each year with the expansion of the city. In today's terms, the case involved billions of dollars.

But all the money was a side issue to Myra Clark Gaines. Her father, an Englishman residing on Esplanade Avenue, had amassed a large fortune in New Orleans land. When he died, his will was either lost or, as Myra contended, destroyed. Unfortunately, the prevailing French law did not require witnesses to such documents, so there was nobody to step up and establish that Clark had intended to leave his property to his daughter, Myra. And so his sly business partners succeeded in cutting her out entirely. Their argument turned on the nasty claim that Myra was illegitimate. Myra obviously disagreed, and insisted that her struggle was solely to vindicate her mother's honor. Since she was wealthy anyway, her claim rings true.

But what is legitimacy? Myra Clark Gaines' mother was a Creole woman named Zulime Carriere. When she married Clark, she thought she was free to do so, for the man to whom she had previously been married turned out to have already had a wife. Zulime and Clark both understood that the first marriage had been annulled according to the Church's laws and the Napoleonic Code. Clark's business partners thought otherwise.

It was touch and go. In one case the court found that Myra was the legitimate child of Clark, in the next case that she was not, and in the two following cases that she was. Meanwhile, so much of the city of New Orleans was being built on Clark's former land that it daily became more improbable that the legacy could ever be turned back to his daughter, even if it was hers by right.

In the end she did not regain her property. But thanks to her case, Myra Clark Gaines' life had the coherence and focus of a Balzac novel. And thanks to her case, too, she became a leading authority on inheritance law generations before there were women lawyers in America.

This is not to say, of course, that true tenacity must always go unrewarded in the Crescent City. For what is most important is that after fifty-six years in the courts, the matter of *Gaines vs. New Orleans* was actually settled. And that's saying something.

SCHISM

For a city that strains every nerve to gain unity and concensus, New Orleans certainly has produced its share of schisms. Coalitions split in two, organizations rupture, and congregations fracture with astonishing frequency. It is like watching a mass of unicellular and jelly-like *amoebae* wiggling under the microscope as they divide and then divide again.

The Biblical view of this phenomenon is that two is better than one anyway. With this authorization from the Divinity, New Orleanians have at various times created two rival ballet companies, two opera guilds, two federated garden clubs, two contending organizations of friends of the zoo, and two cancer societies. During the dark era of Reconstruction there were even two governors and two legislatures, both sworn in on the same day. And in 1934 the mayor, T. Semmes "Turkey Head" Walmsley, raised a squadron of four hundred special policemen, equipped them with machine guns and stationed them around city hall to resist another army of guardsmen sent in to the city by a hostile governor?

The dual governments are gone now, although the sitting mayor, Mr. Morial, and his predecessor, Mr. Landrieu, both Democrats, preside over informal networks of cronies that compete in real estate development schemes and the bidding on amusement parks. On a more significant level, there are still two gourmet establishments run by different branches of the Brennan family. Not to be outdone, the Manale family a few years ago broke into three contending factions, each with its own fine restaurant. And why shouldn't three be better than two?

The quintessential schism is one in which the initial causes of the rupture have long been forgotten by all parties involved. How many Catholics can explain the *filioque* controversy that led to the split between the eastern and western churches in 863 A.D.? In much the same way, the Illinois Club, a distinguished black social organization founded in 1895, became the "Original Illinois Club" when the "Young Men's Illinois Club" declared its independence in 1927. Today no one remembers for sure what happened back then, but the two groups are not about to recombine.

What separates them? Certainly not doctrine, for the only discernible point of difference is that the Original group does a dance step called the "Chicago Glide" at its balls and functions, while the Young Men's group does not.

A second characteristic of the well-honed schism is that everyone involved has to believe devoutly that their differences are infinitely more important than anything they may have in common, and than whatever might set them all off from the rest of mankind. New Orleans politics epitomizes this trait. As in many southern cities, there are a few Republicans around, not to mention Prohibitionists, Whigs, and Flat-Earthers. But the real action is among the Democrats. Indeed, it easy to forget that when two mayoral candidates relentlessly abuse each other they are probably both Democrats, and presumably united in their opposition to Republicans.

Schism being a theological term, it is fitting that this discussion end on a more lofty note than ward politics. According to the Church Fathers, for schism to exist there must be separation on both the spiritual and visible planes. Here is the point where most Crescent City schisms bog down. New Orleanians are seasoned pros at producing highly visible and even audible splits in their ranks, but on the spiritual level they are failures. Leaving aside the Chicago Glide, which is undeniably a serious bone of contention, not one of the current local schisms is genuinely convincing at the level of substance. Which is why every one of them is probably fated to endure into the next millenium.

CORRUPTION

In one of his more prescient statements, William C. Claiborne, who was sent by Thomas Jefferson to look after the newly-purchased territory of Louisiana, wrote President Madison: "Sir, the more I become acquainted with the inhabitants of this Province, the more I am convinced of their unfitness for representative Government . . . [due to] the machinations of the few base individuals."

Nine score years later, those "few base individuals" are still at it. A while back, an otherwise respected state senator from New Orleans was indicted by a federal grand jury for fraud in connection with several bank loans he made through third parties. At the sentencing, the judge told the senator that "the tragedy of this case is...you are convinced beyond any doubt that you have done nothing wrong."

The State Ethics Commission expressed laudable indignation at the senator's maneuvers. Could this have been the same Ethics Comission that only a few weeks earlier had ruled that it was quite all right for public officials to accept gifts from lobbyists, provided they do not actually solicit them? It was. Meanwhile, a former head of this very commission was resting in a federal penitentiary after being indicted in the cloak-and-dagger ABSCAM investigations.

Doesn't the script at this point call for the state's attorney general to ride up on a white horse and uphold virtue? Yes, but alas, just when he was needed, that gentleman was busy preparing his ruling that vote-buying be downgraded from a felony to a misdemeanor.

Evil being universal among mankind, it is a cheap shot to catalogue a few cases of corruption on the lower Mississippi and then damn everyone. After all, it could happen anywhere, and does. The point at issue is not whether wantonness and venality exist, but what kinds and how much. New Orleanians have dabbled in practically every form of civic wickedness over the centuries, but of all its types, the most common corrupt practice today is nepotism.

Robert Bodet, for example, was for many years a hard-working member of the Causeway Commission, the body that oversees the twenty-seven mile-long bridge over Lake Pontchartrain. In his eagerness to get people of his own high calibre on the group's advisory board, Bodet saw to it that his brother and business partner were appointed to it.

In the end, Bodet was sacked—which may be the only unusual feature of his case—only to be immediately reinstated. Usually uncles hire cousins, cousins appoint in-laws, in-laws employ nephews and nephews turn to uncles for help. The music goes round and round, for New Orleans is a family town.

How common is all this? To a man, every current office-holder insists that such deals are far less common now than in the dark past. And they are undoubtedly right, for modern communications are eroding the old covert ways of doing business. But it must be admitted that the public at large still assumes that nepotism and graft are the rule rather than the exception. Why else would a candidate for the post of civil sheriff in New Orleans campaign on the promise that he would not employ a single member of his own family? Heaven knows what such a revolutionary might do if actually elected!

CIVICS LESSON

Students of human folly generally divide into two camps—those who blame it on man's inborn nature and those who place the blame on nurture. The problem with tracing all folly to human nature is that the level of folly is not everywhere the same. If all people are equally prone to folly, then we should expect public morality in New Orleans and Minneapolis to be identical, which is not the case. On the other hand, if you place your cards on nurture—on the corrupting environment—then you must explain why speculation and other such evils have persisted over several centuries in New Orleans, centuries during which this city experienced fundamental changes in its political structure, economy, culture, and even language. Why, in other words, can any present-day New Orleanian, American in language and culture, recognize at once the charge, made in the 1790's by a Frenchman named du Breuil, that all contracts locally were made "under the chimney?"

Corruption endures not because it is an automatic spin-off of the "objective" environment, but because it is an art, one that is passed down through the generations like lace-making or violin-playing. This art is preserved on the lower Mississippi because daily life in New Orleans is a constant civics lesson in reverse, a school for scandal in which all too many students receive marks of "A."

You could watch this alternative school in action at a recent meeting of the St. Bernard Parish Police Jury, an elective body that would elsewhere be called a county council. At this particular meeting a juror named Landry complained about being excluded from membership in the influential Finance Committee. A stormy debate ensued, the point at issue being the rights of an electoral minority. Landry's faction had recently lost control of the Jury but it remained powerful. It therefore tried to claim what it believed to be the legitimate rights of part of the electorate.

193

Instead, it was denied any voice at all.

A member of the majority faction patiently explained to poor Landry how the spoils systems works: "The majority rules . . . and unfortunately, right now you're not in the majority." Expanding on this theme, the Jury president announced that Landry was left off all committees "because of politics." "Politics is how we got here. I didn't do it because you're Floyd Landry; I did it because you were in opposition to us."

As it happened, a civics class from the local high school had chosen this day to attend the session. Turning to the students, the president gave them a proper civics lesson, New Orleans style: "If you're going to fool with politics, boys, you better not think you're in Sunday school; politics is politics...." And so another generation was indoctrinated in the art of spoilsmanship.

Many members of the public understand that they should grab what they can, when they can. This readiness to milk the system for all it's worth pops up in the most unlikely places. Take, for example, the meal bills run up by members of local grand juries. Over an entire year citizen-jurors in the city of New Orleans charged meals at an average of twenty-five dollars each. Amazed, a city council member asked if "they go where they want and order Dom Perignon if they want to?" "Yes," replied the district attorney.

And so they do. One group of twenty-two jurors took their dinner at Antoine's and ran up a bill of $1,188.58, or about fifty-four dollars per member. Moved by their sense of civic responsibility, however, they decided to forgo the Dom Perignon. They did not fail to dig into the filet mignons, however, or the special crab dishes, escargot, and exotic appetizers. And they all finished off with Baked Alaska.

As it happened, these very grand jurors had been empanelled to look into a particularly nasty case of drug smuggling in St. Bernard Parish in which local officials directly responsible to Mr. Landry's police jury were implicated.

SUSPENSE

Happy is the craftsman who masters the skills of his trade. Such a person knows the contentment of a job well done, that sense of self-worth that transcends public plaudits. Such a man was Mr. Henry Meyer of New Orleans' Carrollton section. Until the last years of his career in the early 1930's Meyer practiced his craft with chaste modesty, his artistry unknown even to his neighbors around the corner of Zimpel and Dante streets. But Meyer was, quite literally, irreplaceable. When he died, his craft died with him, the victim of modern technology.

Henry Meyer was the local hangman. Crime was high and convictions were rarely appealed. When Ada LeBoeuf and her lover Dr. Dreher, conspired to murder Mr. LeBoeuf, it eventually fell to Henry Meyer to mete out justice. When the heinous murderers Daleo and Capacci, terrors of the Bridgedale section of Metairie, were finally caught, it was Henry who settled society's score with them. He was a busy man.

Justice is a round-the-clock business. Once, a convicted criminal attempted suicide in his jail cell in order to steal a march on Henry Meyer. It was 3:00 a.m. but the cry went up to "call Henry." Meyer was on the spot by 4:00 a.m., measuring out the rope. The strains must have been enormous.

Besides vigor, the hangman's art requires several skills as well. Henry had acquired a mastery of intricate knots while working as a boatman on the Mississippi. As a carpenter he could also provide useful advice on the design of gallows, such as those in the Gretna jail across the river, or at the corner of Tulane and Rampart streets. But it was Meyer's sure knowledge of the tensile strength of rope that most distinguished him. Whenever a hanging had to be performed, Henry would be there long before the appointed hour, carrying out test runs with sand bags of the appropriate weight. Such tests also worked the stretch out of the rope, so the final performance would be neat and flawless. So adept was Henry Meyer that he could carry out multiple hangings of two, three, or even four felons at once.

It must have required great self-restraint not to gloat publicly about such formidable skills with the noose. But Henry kept his silence. He might even have died anonymously had his identity not been given away by his large, greying handlebar moustache.

Henry's anonymity was lost because the local press just loved hangings. Reporters always came around to watch and they invariably brought their staff photographers with them. Now, Henry Meyer wore a black mask on the job. It was one of those half-masks devised centuries ago for parties in Venice rather than the traditional full-face hood of the hangman. Meyer's mask thus left his elegant mustache exposed to the prying cameras. Little by little, observant folks in Carrollton figured out that Henry was far more than a mere carpenter.

Unfortunately, the resulting notoriety led to some unseemly bravado on Meyer's part during his declining years. At the time of the LeBoeuf hanging, a neighbor named Bubba asked for and received a piece of the fatal rope as a souvenir. Another time, during a heated poker game on the front steps, Henry threatened his recalcitrant opponent with the noose. This was not considered funny.

The rising glare of notoriety and the exhausting work schedule eventually took their toll. Slip-ups began to occur. One of the worst and, for Henry, the most humiliating, occurred during the double hanging of the above-mentioned Messrs. Daleo and Capacci. Miscalculating his distances, Henry dropped them both too far. They were nearly decapitated and Henry's reputation for clean craftsmanship was tarnished. He took to drinking. Down at the parish prison they began talking about the newly-invented electric chair. Soon Henry's carpentry business fell off, too, for craftsmanship is craftsmanship. Hunger set in. Up and down Dante Street it was rumored that the infernal Henry Meyer was stealing milk and bread off people's front stoops in the morning.

It happens to surgeons, concert violinists, hangmen. From one day to the next their skills vanish. Where once there was consummate mastery, there is now only palsied clumsiness. This was Henry Meyer's fate.

New Orleans is a city without a trace of sentiment. When Henry Meyer lost his touch he was out, period. Soon they were installing high-voltage outlets at every one of Henry's former work places. Another handcraft had died.

AN EARNEST EPILOGUE

In which the reader
confronts the wisdom of the
Spanish savant, Ortega y Gasset:
"Tell me what you pay attention to,"
he wrote, "and I'll tell you
who you are."

The Freaks of Fable

Fat Tuesday: Marching to a Different Drummer

AN EARNEST EPILOGUE

Gentle reader, have you finally overcome your insomnia and begun slipping into Lethe's realm? Has the thundering IRT train arrived at your station deep under Manhattan? Are neighbors from the other summer cottage next door scratching urgently at your screened porch to tell you that the steaks are nearly burned? Have the effects of last night's office party finally passed through your weary system?

If so, it is time to conclude these sketches. But they are far from complete. Any native-born New Orleanian will assure you that few of what he knows to be the most important topics concerning the city have been so much as mentioned herein. Even casual tourists from Caracas or Copenhagen will wonder why so many of the matters that aroused their curiosity in the Crescent City have not found a place in these pages.

Such criticism is justified. What possible excuse can there be for passing over such timeless themes as the unlikely Japanese gardens of Pass Christian, the legions of pool halls along Airline Highway, the metaphysical men's room graffiti of St. Bernard Parish, or the strange tribal customs emerging among the staid denizens of One Shell Square, a most chic office complex? None, of course.

Much has been missed. Is it accidental that the city is shaped like a petrie dish, one of those glass laboratory containers in which the most diverse and exotic biological cultures grow and multiply unimpeded by the ordinary limits of nature? The physical resemblance is striking, with the rim formed by the levees and ridges and the fertile spawning zone defined by the central area of Orleans Parish. And as in the laboratory, the closer one peers at New Orleans, the greater the number of unexplained mysteries that appear.

It is one thing to identify unexplored topics and unexamined mysteries but it is quite another matter to discover their significance. William Faulkner referred to New Orleans as "that city foreign and paradoxical." A special kind of vision is needed to decipher it. Otherwise, experiencing New Orleans is like watching an old 3-D movie without the special cardboard-framed glasses that were issued out in the foyer near the popcorn machine. Everything will be a blur, a chaos of out-of-focus images.

The search for that special quality of vision has gone on for a long time. Many people have believed they possess it. The result is an inundation of treatises and books by native and foreign-born observers intent on "exposing" the city of New Orleans. In truth, no other city on the North American continent has been so frequently and so mercilessly stripped bare in print.

Let us speak only of one randomly selected decade, from 1845 to 1855. The yield was typical. Those were the days when French writers were titillating audiences with books on *Les mystères de Paris*. Not to be outdone, a Philadelphian, Edward Carroll Judson, published his own study on *The Mysteries and Miseries of New Orleans* (Philadelphia, 1851). That same year a New Yorker painted himself into the picture with his *A Manhattaner in New Orleans* (New York, 1851). Obviously, to such people New Orleans was not merely a city but a problem to be mulled over and explained.

Given their objectives, it is the more curious to observe the number of authors addressing that problem who sheepishly chose to hide their own identities. Some, like the author of *New Orleans As I Found It in 1845,* coyly adopted a *nom de plume* for the assignment (in this case Henry Didimus). Others, like the author of the forthright *New Orleans As It Is* (New York, 1855), did not even try to hide their shyness. One wonders what their "research" consisted of.

The flow of exposés, revelations, and self-revelations inspired by New Orleans has never flagged with the passage of time. It continues unabated, as the present collection attests. What all the more successful "exposés" have in common is their authors' impatience with mere facts. A century ago a Mr. Bennett Dowles managed to learn everything worth knowing about the geography, business, and even the sewage of New Orleans. But he knew better than to presume that the facts speak for themselves. They don't. And so Dowles published not a dry statistical handbook but *Tableaux* (there's the key) *Geographical, Commercial, Geological and Sanitary* (imagine this one) *of New Orleans* (New Orleans, 1851).

Dowles understood what the mere chronicler is frequently blind to: that individual bits of lively information cannot be forced to stand immobile and harmless on the page. Facts cannot be controlled, yet unchaperoned facts are dangerous. They mingle with other facts around them and soon begin dancing with unlikely partners, cavorting in a most unseemly manner like drunken midwesterners at the quadroon balls back in the 1840's. Then anything can happen. Fortunately, the tableau is more important than the solitary and inert fact anyway. Nothing exists in isolation. What is distinctive emerges only from the confusion of the whole.

Not only is the collection woefully incomplete, like a five-course meal lacking both salad and dessert, but, worst of all, it lacks a solid core of Significant Conclusions—i.e., the main course. In a lame and last-ditch effort to make up for this grievous shortcoming, *let it be suggested* (the passive voice is just what's needed here) that the uniqueness of New Orleans among American cities is its *specific* character, not the fact that it has any character at all. For American cities are by no means so uniform and standardized as they sometimes appear to be on the surface. The resident of Seattle may well be glued to the same televised football games and soap operas as his or her counterpart in Montpelier or Roanoke, but don't think for a minute that their worlds are otherwise interchangeable. For they're not.

Back in the administration of Franklin D. Roosevelt, the Works Projects Administration (WPA) tried to pin down the distinctive features of all our major cities in its still useful series of guides. A similar effort today might not produce so rich a lode of material, but it would be very rewarding nonetheless. It would remind us that even in the age of computers, each human community possesses its own characteristic features, many of them formed over decades and even centuries. Practical people know that they can ignore such elements only at their peril. Wise people, moreover, realize that to appreciate and participate in a richly-textured communal existence is one of the greatest pleasures that life affords.

So much for Signicant Conclusion Number One. Should there be a second, a third? Here the pen hesitates. The thick, wet heat of a New Orleans summer presses in through the open door, carrying the sound of a dog barking at a fence post down the street somewhere. Everything slows down. The mind wanders out the door and down the street. Its last thought, as it permits the hand to release the pen, is of Binx Bolling, the existential hero of Walker Percy's New Orleans novel, *The Moviegoer*, who philosophizes that "any serious search for meaning must begin with an examination of man's seemingly invincible apathy." Well put, Binx!

Bemused, the brain briefly revives and, as it processes the pleasant impressions of the night's stillness, recalls the words of another writer, this time Henry Bradsher Fearon, a British traveller who visited the Crescent City in 1819, probably on a night just like this:

To all men whose desire only is to live a short life but a
merry one, I have no hesitation in recommending New Orleans.

The End.

THE AUTHOR

S. Frederick Starr is President of Oberlin College. He wrote *New Orleans UnMasqued* during the wagwit's occupancy of New Orleans as Vice President for Academic Affairs, Tulane University, Scholar-in-Residence at the Historic New Orleans Collection, and clarinetist for the Louisiana Repertory Jazz Ensemble, founded by Starr.

Starr is highly regarded for his knowledge in foreign affairs and has served as Secretary of the Kennan Institute for Advanced Russian Studies at the Wilson Center in Washington, D.C. He is the author of several previously released books, including *Red and Hot: The Fate of Jazz in the Soviet Union* (Oxford), *Melnikov: Solo Architect in a Mass Society* (Princeton), and *The Russian Avant Garde: The George Costakis Collection* (Abrams).

THE ARTIST

Franklin Adams is a painter, sculptor and designer, born in 1933 in Jacksonville, Florida, but an adopted New Orleanian since he arrived in 1958 to teach in the Department of Art of Tulane University's Newcomb College. In 1978 he transferred to Tulane's School of Architecture, where he is presently Associate Professor of Architecture. He can't remember whether he first met Fred Starr in the halls of academe or at the Maple Leaf Bar dancing to Starr's virtuoso clarinet in the Louisiana Repertory Jazz Ensemble.